THE NURSERY AGE CHILD

The Karnac Developmental Psychology Series

Published and distributed by Karnac Books

Other titles in the Series

The 5–10-year-old Child
  Abrahão H. Brafman

Orders

Tel: +44 (0)20 7431 1075; Fax: +44 (0)20 7435 9076

E-mail: shop@karnacbooks.com

www.karnacbooks.com

THE NURSERY AGE CHILD

Jenny Davids

First published in 2010 by
Karnac Books Ltd
118 Finchley Road, London NW3 5HT

British Library Cataloguing in Publication Data

A C.I.P. for this book is available from the British Library

ISBN: 978 1 85575 795 0

Edited, designed and produced by The Studio Publishing Services Ltd
www.publishingservicesuk.co.uk
e-mail: studio@publishingservicesuk.co.uk

www.karnacbooks.com

CONTENTS

ACKNOWLEDGEMENTS

Heartfelt thanks to Dr Abe Brafman for asking me to write this book and bearing with me with much patience. You have been a true facilitator to a journey that has had many twists and turns.

The encouragement and interest of friends has been vital, and I would like to thank Alison Adie, Hilda Brockbank, Julien Ben-hamou, Sheila Chait, Tony Fagin, Anne Hurry, Glenda Levin, Mike Lodrick, Norka Malberg, Hilda and Jonathan Matheson, Fran Michelman, Philip Stanbridge, and Eileen Wilkins.

I am grateful to colleagues who have allowed me to use vig-nettes. Special mention to Jennifer Johns, Tamsin Ford and Hazel Marsh.

A special thank you to Donald Campbell, who has been there through the twists and the turns.

Finally, to the children I have known as a therapist and as friends—thank you for letting me in to your worlds, and allowing me to join in some of your sense of discovery.

To C. C. R. B

ABOUT THE AUTHOR

Jenny Davids trained as a clinical psychologist in Cape Town, where she worked as a research fellow in the Department of Psychology at the University of Cape Town. She then trained in child and adolescent psychoanalysis and psychotherapy at the Anna Freud Centre. She was a member of staff there for twenty years, enjoying clinical work and teaching. She also worked as a child and adolescent psychotherapist in the National Health Service, at the Middlesex hospital and in community paediatrics. She was a consultant child psychotherapist and clinical lead of a team for looked-after children in the South London and Maudsley Trust. She was a training supervisor for the Anna Freud Centre, and is a supervisor and teacher at the British Association of Psychotherapists. More recently, Jenny has developed her interest in adult work and completed her training in adult psychoanalysis at the Institute of Psychoanalysis. Currently, she is a member of the British Psychoanalytic Society and is in private practice in London, working with children, adolescents, and adults.

SERIES EDITOR'S FOREWORD

Searching for a trustworthy nursery school for your three-year-old child can be a time of considerable anxiety. Indeed, a developmental step you had been looking forward to, but for most families this also represents an end to the years when the child spent all the day in the home, and the day when you have to say good-bye to the child at the school's gate can be a testing experience. This is the first major step towards the child's discovery of the world outside his nuclear family.

For the child, the period between three and five years of age brings a continuous flow of discoveries: people, places, activities, a plethora of new experiences. And the child has to learn how to accommodate the two worlds in which he lives. A challenge for the child and a challenge for the parents!

In this book, Jenny Davids draws on her rich years of work with children and parents to describe the many areas of life where we can admire and enjoy—and, at times, worry over—the child's progress in his physical and emotional development. The examples she quotes are most illuminating and helpful. Ms Davids worked for many years as a child psychotherapist and is now a psychoanalyst of adults and children. She has published a number of papers on her work, and we are pleased that she has contributed to this series of books.

The literature describing the developmental stages that lead the infant to adulthood contains two aspects that deserve to be made explicit and discussed. One is the difference between references to the *actual* infant, as distinct from those focusing on the *reconstructed* infant (Stern, 1995); the other follows from this one and involves the degree of experience that the authors have of direct, close involvement with infants and children. It is very easy to ignore these features, but, once aware of them, one realizes how important they are and the degree to which they affect the views put forward by the authors.

Over the years, I have met many analysts and psychotherapists to discuss the observation of infants or actual clinical work with children. I came to recognize that some of these students or qualified professionals spoke about the infant or child they were involved with in a manner that suggested a sense of distance and coldness; they seemed to be reporting the finding of something they had read or heard about. I could not pick up the tone of delight and warmth that one experiences when discovering something new in an object that one feels close to, the sense of excitement and discovery that an individual object engenders when approached with a background of recognition and familiarity. In other words, having been close to other infants or children, the gratifying discovery that this is not "just another infant", but a new, different, special infant, with his own unique characteristics.

Eventually, it occurred to me to ask these students what previous experience they had had with young children and I was surprised to find that the infant they observed or the child they were treating was the first child they had ever come so close to. These were professionals who had trained to work with adults, and it became clear that the images they had of "an infant" or "a child" had been gained from their studies. I later found that most people who decided to train in the analytic approach to children opted for the child psychotherapy training, while those who chose the psychoanalytic training were aiming to work with adults. This may well be the explanation for the failure of all the efforts made by so many analysts to persuade their trainees to get involved with children or, at least, with the study of children.

Anna Freud (1972) saw the child as a live field of research and she believed that "child analysis . . . opened up the possibility to check up on the correctness of reconstructions in adult analysis" (p. 153). And yet,

> analysts of adults remained more or less aloof from child analysis, almost as if it were an inferior type of professional occupation . . . It was difficult not to suspect that most analysts vastly preferred the childhood images which emerged from their interpretations to the real children in whom they remained uninterested. [*ibid.*]

Hannah Segal (1972) shared Anna Freud's views:

> In our institute in Great Britain we had for years lectures on child analysis and clinical seminars, which were compulsory for all students. Unfortunately, we are going through one of our periodic great upheavals and reorganization, and I find to my horror that the child has been thrown out with the bath water: the course of child analysis for the ordinary candidate has disappeared, I hope only very temporarily. [p. 160]

To help a professional to obtain true, thorough familiarity with the growing child, she listed what she saw as her

> minimal requirements: first, full integration of theory of psycho-analytic knowledge derived from the analysis of children in teach-ing; secondly, baby and child observation; and thirdly, attendances at lectures and clinical seminars on child analysis irrespective of whether the candidate is treating children himself. [*ibid.*]

In fact, infant observation has been the only one of these disci-plines that has been (virtually) universally adopted as part of the training in adult analysis and psychotherapy. However, analysing the reports of students and reading the available literature, we can recognize the effect of the preconceptions with which the observers approach infant and parent(s). We can only *see* what *we make* of that which our eyes show us. This is not pathological; it is an inevitable fact. Whichever one of our senses is stimulated, some perception is formed and immediately interpreted in line with previous experi-ences. Presumably, each and every one of us is able to spot a sen-sorial stimulus not previously met, but if some stop and try to make sense of it, others quickly ignore it, choosing to concentrate on more familiar perceptions and interpretations. Of course, nobody reaches adulthood without having been involved with children of all ages, but there is a major difference between taking an interest, developing a relationship, and warming up to children and, instead, approaching children as no more than an object of study.

Friends, colleagues, acquaintances, relatives of all ages arouse feelings and images of various degrees of clarity in our minds and we are usually able to describe their qualities and attributes as individuals. But, on becoming a student, there is a powerful qualitative change in our frame of mind and we move on to learn about and search for group characteristics; indeed, this is a response to what most teachers expect from their trainees. In zoology, we learn of species, races, genders, etc., much as in psychology we discover all kinds of classifications of appearance, behaviours, etc. Since medicine has "diagnosis" as the primary goal in the process of investigation of the individual patient, the student has to work hard to learn the relevant data to consider when making his "differential diagnosis", i.e., having considered all *possible* illnesses that *might* be affecting that particular individual, deciding which one is, in fact, producing the clinical phenomena found in that particular patient.

And here lies the problem I wanted to define and focus on. Meeting an infant or a child, we are flooded with images and possible interpretations of what *that child*'s appearance, behaviour, utterances, etc., are supposed to indicate. But, having examined each and every one of these *impressions*, we still have to admit that these are no more than interpretations based on our previous life experiences. Only a closer interaction with the particular child will help us to clarify which of our hypotheses are in fact correct, and, at last, recognize and define the specific cluster of conscious and unconscious thoughts and emotions experienced by the child that lead to its expressed, manifest behaviour and utterances.

The reports of students on their observations of infants demonstrate very clearly the degree to which their descriptions reflect the theoretical framework they are being trained in. Indeed, their personal opinions also influence what they perceive, and only when they give a detailed enough description of their observations will other students be able to recognize other possible ways of interpreting what has been observed. Two examples may illustrate this point:

A seven-month-old baby was described as particularly unresponsive to the mother's ministrations. The student, in fact, at times considered the mother's behaviour as a possible cause of the baby's responses. Taking a broader view of the three visits under discussion, the other students in the group questioned the assessment of their colleague. After some discussion, it occurred to me to ask whether he might be considering the baby's behaviour as an early sign of autism; rather hesitantly, he admitted this was the case. This led to a major change in the focus of the discussion. Subsequent visits led to reports of a normally developing baby, with a mother who seemed to treat him in a very normal manner.

A ten-week-old baby was described as "attacking the mother's nipple in an oral sadistic" manner and, accordingly, producing pain and a withdrawal reaction in the mother. When the student visited the family the following week, the baby was reported as sucking quite normally the mother's breast. The students in the group were, obviously, puzzled, and asked about the destructive oral instincts of the baby. The reporting student, rather timidly, answered that the mother had been visited a few days earlier by a breastfeeding counsellor.

As infants learn to speak and to convey their feelings in a more understandable manner, it becomes easier to make contact with them and gradually learn to understand how they are experiencing life in the world around them. But, predictably, this is easier said than done! Parents, teachers, and doctors find it much easier to TELL the child what they think than to find a way of enabling the child to express what, in fact, are his experiences. Teaching, reassuring, ignoring, comforting, pacifying—or punishing—a child is infinitely easier than conveying to that child that one is interested in discovering what is exciting, worrying, bothering, or frightening him/her.

The parents of a twelve-year-old boy were worried by his behaviour, his refusal to discuss anything with them. School reports were satisfactory, but the parents worried that the boy might be developing some kind of pathological aloofness. I saw the boy on his own and found no sign of the behaviour reported by the parents. I suggested to the parents that I should meet the boy a few more times, but I reassured them that I had not detected any indication of incipient pathology in their son. I wondered whether the behaviour at home might be a pattern developed within the child–parents relationship and inquired what image they had of their interactions with the boy in his earlier years. After some thought, the father recounted that when the boy was four years old he told him one day that he "knew that God created the earth". Father said this was good and continued doing what he was involved with. But, after a few minutes, the boy asked him, "Do you want me to tell you how it is that I know?" The father felt embarrassed, and asked the boy to tell him. "Because there was no ground for any-one to stand on, so only a God could have done it". I suggested that that episode might have remained in the boy's mind as a warning that, in principle, his father was not interested to learn of his thoughts.

If I had only seen the boy by himself, I would not have heard of this episode. Individual sessions would probably reveal his inability to feel free and spontaneous when addressing his father and per-haps he might be helped not to extend this sense of intimidation to his relationship with other men. But if the father can realize the impact his responses have on his son, this may lead him to develop a different pattern of responses to the son. Broadening our picture, we have here examples of keeping an open mind when approaching a child and his parents. The student who thought he was observing an autistic child could recognize the extent to which his initial impressions were influencing his subsequent analysis of his data; the student who thought she had found evidence of Klein's theories regarding the destructive aspects of the oral instincts could take into account the subsequent piece of evidence that strongly argued against her interpretation of the baby's behaviour. The memory put forward by the father of the twelve-year-old boy is a powerful piece of evidence of the importance at all ages of environmental factors shaping a child's mode of relating to his environment.

These arguments and examples aim to depict an approach to child development where the emphasis is on the actual personal experience of each child and his parents, rather than on a particu-lar body of theories built to explain human development. The emphasis is on the richness and freedom that a sense of doubt can create, rather than on the advocacy of dogmatic certainty. Instead of starting from the theoretical and searching for the evi-dence that will substantiate it, we are choosing an approach where we aim to understand the personal experience of the child and of his parents, and gradually build a picture of the development of their interactions.

The concept of instinctual impulses is well accepted in all areas of biology, but in the analytic world it has become attached to other psychoanalytic concepts to an extent that, to my mind, is difficult to justify. For example, the concepts of self and object images are most useful to evaluate the level of development of an infant's ego, but when it is postulated that instincts can influence the formation of object images *in utero*, I consider this the type of hypothesis that demands faith for its acceptance, since we do not have the equipment to evaluate its validity. The episode quoted above of the observer who claimed to have found evidence of how hostile impulses had led an infant to attack its bad maternal object is an example of this particular application of the concept of inborn instincts.

The opposite extreme is represented by the theories that claim that the infant's personality is the result of the environment in which he grows up. Needless to say, all of these theories will always include comments on the importance of other factors in shaping the infant's development, but not much notice is given to these "other" factors in the description of the developing infant and child. Predictably, analysts will develop their clinical approach in line with the theoretical framework they favour. For example, analysts who maintain that psychopathology originates from early infancy mothering will see early developmental pathology in the patient's material and, correspondingly, attempt to offer a more effective mothering experience.

The authors of the books in this series follow a balanced view of these various theories. There is a refreshing lack of dogmatic views and a high dose of good sense, where theories are respected and quoted, always making sure that a reader can find enough material to form his own view on the validity of the interpretations put forward.

Each book in this series focuses on a particular age range of a child's development. The emphasis is on the description of the typical ways in which the child, at each of these stages, experiences himself in his world. As he develops, the child has different needs, abilities, and resources that underlie his interaction with parents, relatives, and the world at large. Our objective is to illustrate how these unfolding characteristics of the child influence and are influenced by the people in his world. It is only careful and (usually) long-term observation that will allow us to identify elements in the infant's or child's behaviour that are likely to be part of his inborn personality.

Whenever considering a particular individual, it is not difficult to put forward hypotheses about the origins of his various characteristic features, but the converse is virtually impossible. However refined our powers of observation, we are quite incapable of predicting what effects the course of time will produce on an individual. Here lies the special fascination of studying infants and children, where all the time we are surprised by some piece of behaviour we would not have managed to predict.

Meeting the child and his parents, we have to explore the patterns of the relationship they have with each other, and it is virtually impossible to establish what is cause and what is effect in the way they treat each other. Through their words and behaviour, child and parents continuously confirm each other's expectations and keep a self-perpetuating vicious circle going, where each of them feels totally justified in his/her views of him/herself and each other. However, if we find a way of enabling a child to reveal his private thoughts and feelings, we can sometimes discover that these do not quite match his usual statements: most children learn to sense and respect how each parent expects them to behave and what to say, when and where.

All the authors in this series follow a theoretical framework that maintains the importance of emotional and intellectual factors of which we may be unconscious at a particular time. They also follow the theory that individuals are continuously influenced by their experiences—past and present—both those originating in the person's mind and those resulting from interactions with other people. This approach is referred to as a "dynamic" view of the human personality. However, all our authors are aware of the existence of factors in our make-up that appear not to be amenable to change. In fact, we are privileged in having a specific volume in the series that addresses the issue of disadvantage. Given appropriate professional help, such children can improve their capacity to deal with life, but in many cases it will be difficult to predict the extent of this change and, equally important, to determine whether the child acquires new coping mechanisms or, instead, structural changes are achieved.

These differences are significant, not just from a scientific point of view, but also in terms of what we, the professionals, convey to the parents about our assessment of each child. When a child has a structural, inborn or acquired problem, we owe it to the parents to make very clear that, in the course of time, they have learnt of the child's abilities and limitations and found ways of taking these into account when looking after the child. In other words, that some of the child's problems are not the result of their upbringing, but of some factor that is not always easy to pinpoint. When there is no such physical, organic, non-dynamic factor, we can indeed assume we are facing a dynamic problem, but even then it can be difficult to predict the extent to which our therapeutic efforts will achieve change in the presenting problems. This is, in fact, the most difficult challenge that a consultant faces each time he assesses a new child.

It is not rare that each parent will present a quite different reading of what he considers the child's problems to be. Needless to say, the same can be found when considering any issue in the life of an ordinary family. The baby cries and the mother thinks he is hungry, while the father may feel that here is an early warning of a child who will wish to control his parents' lives. The toddler refuses some particular food and the mother resents this early sign of rebellion, while the father will claim that the child is actually showing he can discriminate between pleasant and undesirable flavours. The five-year-old demands a further hour of TV watching and the mother agrees he should share a programme she happens to enjoy, while the father explodes at the pointlessness of trying to instil a sense of discipline in the house. By the time the child reaches puberty or adolescence, these clashes are a matter of daily routine . . . From a practical point of view, it is important to recognize that there is no question of ascertaining which parent is right or which one is wrong: within their personal frame of reference, they are both right. The problem with such disagreements is that, whatever happens, the child will always be agreeing with one of them and opposing the other. But, at this point, I wish to emphasize the obvious fact that each parent reaches his interpretation of the child's behaviour in line with his upbringing and his personality, his view of himself in the world, his past and present experiences, some of which are conscious and most of them unconscious. But—what about the child in question?

It is not part of ordinary family life that a child should be asked what *his* explanation is for the piece of behaviour that led to the situation where the parents disagreed on its interpretation. And, anyway, when he is asked about this, there is a fair chance that, very quickly, one or both parents will challenge him and utter the famous line, "Really? I know your antics! Pull the other one! What you really wanted is . . .". It is just not common to find parents (adults in general, perhaps?) interested and able to discover a child's private justification for his behaviour. Sometimes, the child fails to find the words to explain himself, occasionally he is driven to say what he believes the parent wants to hear, at other times his words sound too illogical to be believed; somehow, the myth has grown that only a professional will have the capacity to fathom out the child's motives and intentions.

Each family will have its own style of approaching their child. It is simply unavoidable that each individual child will have his development influenced (note: not determined, but affected) by the responses his behaviour brings out in his parents. It is, however, quite difficult for parents to appreciate the precise developmental abilities achieved by their child. No child can operate, cope with life, respond to stimuli beyond his particular abilities at any particular point in time. And this is THE point addressed in the present series of books. We try to portray the various stages in the child's cognitive, intellectual, emotional development and how these unfolding stages affect not only his experience of himself, but also how he perceives and responds to the world in which he lives. We hope that this approach will help parents and professionals to gauge how best to make contact with the child and reach an understanding of his feelings and behaviour.

References

Freud, A. (1972). Child analysis as a sub-speciality of psychoanalysis. *International Journal of Psychoanalysis*, 53: 151–156.

Segal, H. (1972). The role of child analysis in the general psychoanalytical training. *International Journal of Psychoanalysis*, 53: 157–161.

Stern, D. (1995). *The Motherhood Constellation*. New York: Basic Books.

Abrahão H. Brafman
Series Editor

Introduction

In this book, my aim is to share some of my understandings of nursery age children, that is, children around three, four, and five years old, and their parents. Children of these ages have always fascinated me. The wealth of their growing minds is apparent in their play and in their widening capacity to express themselves in words. It is a time of much discovery and experimentation, accompanied often by excitement and anxiety. There is something rather open-minded and open-hearted about children of these years.

My views on nursery age children have been based on observing and working with them over the past twenty years, in various settings, including their homes, nursery schools, and hospitals, and, as a psychologist and child psychotherapist, in assessments and individual psychotherapy. I have also learnt much in working with families and with groups of parents. In my role as consultant to schools, the staff have taught me a great deal and deepened my awareness of children in educational settings.

The writings of Sigmund Freud, Donald and Clare Winnicott, Anna Freud, Selma Fraiberg, and Jean Piaget have influenced and informed my own perspectives.

For the sake of clarity, I refer to the child as he and the parent as she throughout the book.

The period spanning the fourth and sixth year of life is a time when the child faces realities and changes that require emotional strength and, particularly, the capacity to keep struggling with frustration and, to some extent, pain. The parents have a key role in encouraging their children's passage through these years.

The nursery age years are a time when the child is building and adding to his sense of who he is, both as a unique person and as a girl or boy.

It is also a time when parents grow and develop new dimensions of being a parent. Issues such as separation and sleep, which have been around in the baby and toddler years, now present in different guises. The nursery age child may bring new sets of anxieties to these same dilemmas, so the parents need to alter their view of the child's capacities and normal struggles during these years. The active, developing mind of the child needs to be respected by the parent. The thinking and talking of the curious child can be both exciting and demanding to the parent. Parents may find themselves reminded of their own childhoods and may need to become aware of their hidden expectations of their children. Such desires do not necessarily help the parent to promote the unique identity of her child. Parents are faced with the dilemma of how much to encourage their child and how much to stand back; this, of course, depends on the personality and needs of the particular child.

The nursery age child is struggling with the issue of sibling rivalry, and with friendships in the wider family and community. Play is developing both with and without other children, and the parent may be needed to provide and guard a sense of safety as the nursery age child can suddenly become over-stimulated and lose the boundary between pretend and reality.

During these years, the child is developing his sense of himself as a boy or girl. The parents' communication of their pride and pleasure in these aspects of their child's development is vital in the evolution of self-esteem.

The kind of innovation and sense of adventure which often characterizes these nursery age years can form part of the foundation of creativity in later childhood and adult life. Freud and Winnicott have written much about how patterns are established during these years which affect not only creativity, but also who the child is identified with, who he chooses to love in later life, what kind of work he chooses to do, and many personality traits.

I hope that this book captures both the imaginative, fluid world of nursery age children as well as the hard everyday work that parents face in facilitating their growth.

CHAPTER ONE

The child's view of himself

I n some respects, the nursery age child, rather like the toddler, is itching to try new experiences, to carry on exploring the world around him. By *nursery age*, I mean the years ranging from about three to five.

The nursery age child is developing a sense of what he can do; this includes the discovery that "I make an impact on the world and on others", as well a sense of being able to make things happen in a realistic way rather than through purely imaginary play. The child is continuing the profound and crucial process of becoming his own person, a person with his own view/s on things. Such perspectives are characterized by an admixture of fantastic and realistic thinking, the beginnings of reasoning and heartfelt desires. The nursery age child has one foot in the world of magic and fantasy, and the other in the world of reality, testing out how things work and noticing the consequences of his actions.

The young child's thinking and language is developing at a pace. In this way, the child can give shape and meaning to his own experiences and perceptions. Often, there is tremendous excitement and joy in discovering aspects of the self: "I can make up games"; "I can think up stories"; "I can do some things that my sibs and parents do". There is also the key realization of limitations—"what I am not able to do". The nursery age child once again faces the pain of having to work for a skill, or wait for a time when he will be ready to give it a go with more chance of success. When this happens, the child usually looks to those around him to check their reaction. The parent or older sibling or teacher can soften the blow of the disappointments and setbacks discovered on the road to self-expansion. They can help cushion the frustration and sustain the optimistic hope that the child will be successful in the not too distant future—a message of "Oh dear, not now, do try again later", can be given.

The nursery age child is very focused on the discovery of what he can achieve with his body. It is thrilling to discover and experience one's own capacity to move: "I can run, slide, somersault, turn upside down, spin round and round". The child finds the acrobat in himself. He also discovers the limitations of his acrobatic abilities. For example, the discovery that "I cannot twist myself into a shape like one of those animated creatures I see on the television; my body won't do that and I wonder why? I also learn that my body hurts when I fall and graze and knock myself".

> Leon, five years and nine months old, was mortified when he discovered that he could not fly like an aeroplane from the top bunk; he was not so much upset by having broken his arm when he landed as by having to acknowledge that he could not fly. Experiences such as these result in the establishment of a sense of self that is grounded in reality.

Doing is a key element in the building of the child's sense of being. The sense of "what I can do" goes to form part of the experience of "I am", and is also incorporated in the experience of "being with". Doing with and being with are often closely related, especially in the beginnings of the young child's friendships.

The child is developing a sense of a healthy, productive self, of "how I am growing and developing"; and a sense of a solid "I" that can be relied on, of a "me" that will be there to be found tomorrow or, if not, the next day. It is important that the child be encouraged, but not pushed, by the parent to discover, often through "doing" and "being with", his own likes and dislikes as well as his own uncertainties, so that an individuality is created and extended. In a nursery school, one soon gets a feel of the various personalities in the group; parents and teachers soon find themselves enjoying the children's unique sense of themselves.

Some children come across as miniature grown-ups, acting and talking strikingly like an adult. Parents may find this amusing, and in small doses it can be; other parents may sense something uncomfortable about this stance in their child, as if there were something out of kilter. Parents may be contributing in some way, knowingly or unknowingly, to the creation of the miniature adult. It is known that our childhood experiences can influence our later life, and it is, therefore, helpful for parents to think about how they were treated as children. Were they treated subtly or openly as older than their years by their parents? Were they encouraged to emulate their parents and older siblings? Did they have a sibling who insisted on behaving in ways younger than his years? One way of creating a child older than his years is for the parent to turn to the child as a substitute for a partner, for example, when there are substantial absences of a partner or when there are tensions or misunderstandings between the parents as a couple. Some children may find being placed in such a role as flattering and making them feel special. But being put in such a position repeatedly, although understandable when we consider the parent's needs, is not appropriate to the developing child and his needs.

There may be some aspect of her nursery age child's behaviour that the parent finds awkward to relate to and finds herself wanting to minimize or curtail. Some parents treat children almost as equals, talking to them and expecting them to respond like another adult, and perhaps forgetting that their child has different emotional needs and conflicts. As discussed above, early experiences may repeat themselves for the parent who may then need to become aware of her own childhood wishes and needs, and distinguish them from those of her child. An overly intellectual manner, or a sense of talking above the nitty gritty dilemmas, may need reconsidering. Children often imbibe and reproduce such tendencies of the parent without the parent being conscious of her own style and its impact on her child. As a parent, one does not always realize how much one's child is closely observing and absorbing from one, and especially aspects of oneself that one might not be aware of, or, even so, willing to acknowledge. Nursery age children can surprise their parents with their use of the parents' choice of words, and their reproduction of the nuances of the parents' table manners and gestures, to mention a few.

Although some parents may be only too pleased by the child who is not quarrelsome or argumentative, others may become concerned by a tendency in their child to try too hard or to be too good. Parents may ask themselves whether the too good child may be sensing something in the parent and trying to shield the parent from more uncomfortable feelings. For example, the child may be trying to be very good to the parent who is sick. The child may be worried that his actions may have indeed caused the illness; he may fear that he could make his parent worse, and there may be underlying anxieties about even losing his parent. Such a child may be relieved if his parent can talk to him about the child's worries and give the message that the child does not have to walk on eggshells for the sake of the parent.

The child who tries too hard may benefit from a parent who can communicate a genuine sense of perspective and balance, a realistic attitude that you lose some, you win some. Parents may have to re-examine themselves and may be surprised to find very strong competitive wishes in themselves and very high expectations of their children. A driven attitude in the child may be a pointer to insecurity and a worry that he will be perceived by himself and others as unlovable if he is not the best, or near-perfect. Sometimes children pressure themselves in order to gain the attention and love of parents who are felt to be dismissive of them, or experienced as preoccupied with other people or activities. It might be helpful to the child for the parent to pause to think about what her child is trying to communicate and how she might alter her response according to how she understands the child's messages. Parents can help their children manage the disappointment and hurt that may accompany mistakes. A child can be much relieved and comforted by sensing that his parent loves him no matter how successful he is, or how many mistakes he makes.

Unhappiness may show in a number of ways. Some children will withdraw into themselves, while others become overly boisterous, constantly seeking new satisfactions. Somehow, quite often, the withdrawn child will not attract the adults' attention, while the boisterous one will promptly arouse concern. In fact, the withdrawn child may need his parent to draw him out, to engage his interest and capture his attention, much as the boisterous one may need calming, to be shown the limits of acceptable behaviour and, if necessary, even being stopped. As we well know, quite often parents disagree on their assessment of the child's behaviour. Discussions about these differences of opinion can be helpful; parents sometimes feel freer to explore and express their views away from the child, who is often very sensitive to the tensions between his parents. Difficulties can arise when the child does not fit the picture the parent has of him in her mind.

Imagination and play are vital ingredients of the child's existence. They are the fabric of the child's expanding inner world. Some of the fantasies can be shared and, indeed, elaborated with others. It is very important that parents enable the child to share with them his fantasies, rather than simply correcting the child and, thereby, curtailing the child's further voicing of his fantasies.

The nursery age child's fantasies can be welcomed by his playmates. This is a crucial time for the deepening and widening of the child's relationships and social circle. Simply put, a child who has friends usually feels liked and wanted. These good feelings then become part of the child's positive view of himself. He feels himself able to belong and as having something valuable to contribute to others around him. The horizons of his knowledge expand and are enriched by the differing views and perspectives of other children.

CHAPTER TWO

The child's view of the world around him

The nursery age child is venturing out, expanding horizons and building a sense of independence. There is movement away from the orbit of the parents, carers, and the physical confines and rhythms of the home environment.

I observed one three-year-old girl who kept on lagging behind her mum, stopping to explore the world. She was looking intently at the movements of a small beetle. It was if she were saying, "I want to explore at my pace. I want to be captivated by the movements of a little insect finding its way across an uneven pavement. I don't want my concentration interrupted."

And, indeed, this deep concentration and determined focusing of attention plays a vital role in one of the key activities that is becoming more elaborated at this age, which is play with the self and with others.

It is vital for the child's growth that the parents do sometimes step back to allow the space and time for the growing child's curiosity to emerge, to be awakened and sustained. The parent has a difficult task in that she has to learn to hold back and not to intrude or take over the play. She can view the play from a distance and be aware of it, perhaps even interested. If invited in by the child, she would do well to participate by following the child, or wondering alongside the child. She needs to refrain from teaching or correcting. She has to find the patience in herself to wait to be asked, thereby giving her child the freedom and the pride in finding out at his own pace. This sensitive attunement to her child and respect of her child's discovery of the world will pay dividends in the child's development of his own unique creative self.

These excursions into the world, these first discoveries and rediscoveries, are very precious. The child may ask questions about the experience and the parent can help the child by elaborating, providing new knowledge, and by listening to and answering his questions.

The preschool child is often likened to a little philosopher who poses questions about the nature of the universe, about the nature of what we often take for granted or have not thought about deeply. What is a sunbeam? Why does the sea go back? Where does the water in the basin go? What is a cloud? Much is being noticed and puzzled about. Parents sometimes feel that they are being kept on their toes. It is important that parents try to make their answers match the child's true abilities and needs. The "truth" of the adult often goes far beyond the child's understanding.

Alongside all these excursions into the wider world is the child's need to know that the parent remains steadily in the background as backup and support. This knowledge is part of what Bowlby (1988) has written about is his concept of the secure base, the idea of the accessible parent in the child's mind, a safe shelter he can seek and turn to when needed in the midst of his growing independence. The world is a mixed bag for the child. On the one hand, it is immensely thrilling and new, waiting to be discovered. On the other hand, the nursery age child can suddenly shrink back or be brought to a sudden halt by perceiving an aspect of the world he is venturing into as alarming. This is also the age of many fears and phobias.

The nursery age child can become convinced that to step off the carpeted area of the stairs will result in his getting bitten by the monster that the child believes lives on and rules the stairs. The puppy the child had been happily playing with, even looking after, can suddenly become an object of terror when the puppy starts to bark. Parents can adopt various approaches to these fears, some involving a playful approach, others one of reassurance and comfort. A key ingredient should be the parent's attempts to empathize to some extent with the child, but also to help her child find ways through these fears, so that the world does not become an overwhelmingly frightening place. It is important for the parents to realize that such anxieties are part of his learning about the world and are not necessarily a sign of pathology, "something wrong with the child".

There are many parts to the child's new world. He is developing an understanding of his family, who makes it up and its broader structure. He is often developing relationships, not only with his immediate family, but also with his wider family, which can include cousins, aunts and uncles, and, of course, grandparents. He, in himself, is broadening his repertoire of play and so is increasingly more able to join in or be invited to join in with older children. Sometimes, families are somewhat isolated, with relatives living at some distance or even in another country. Long-distance relatives may be known through their photographs, e-mails, or voices over the telephone. Some children take time to become familiar with these absent but present relatives.

Often the community becomes a kind of surrogate family. The child gets to know neighbours, people in the community who share similar cultural and leisure activities with his parents, and friends of the family, including friends of his brothers and sisters. His world is further expanded by attending a nursery school and learning how to relate to teachers and other school staff. Through exposure to the wider community, he comes to meet and know children and families of different cultures and religions, who speak various languages, and who hold diverse opinions and beliefs. The parents' views and comments about these people will definitely influence how the nursery age child comes to see them. Parents often underestimate just how much the child observes and copies their attitudes and words about unfamiliar people who speak and behave differently. Children may use expressions that the parents are then surprised to discover they have been using themselves.

CHAPTER THREE

Discoveries and discovering

My view of development is that it follows a zig-zag path, with spurts forward alternating with slips backwards. It does not proceed smoothly in one direction; there are backward slips, falls, and sometimes phases of hesitation, rest, and even of no movement. Growth and development require much courage; worries often accompany taking new steps, although excitement may also be found in the jumps into the new. The child who is caught up in the minutiae of fear, doubt, and hesitation may be helped by the parents' longer-term view, whose eye is on the end in sight. The nursery age child experiences these pulls forwards and the pushes backwards; what needs to be kept in mind by the parent is the overall forward movement, that progress is usually superseding staying still or falling backwards.

Donald Winnicott, a paediatrician and psychoanalyst, wrote of the complex sides of the child's personality: his is a multi-dimensional view. Winnicott writes,

> . . . each child of four is also three and also two and also one, and is also an infant being weaned, or an infant just born, or even an infant in the womb. *Children go backwards and forwards in their emotional age.* [Winnicott, 1964, p. 179, my italics]

It is this dynamism and movement that makes these early years so exciting and challenging. The young child is experiencing the world for the first time, discovering the world anew. Parents sometimes say that this is part of the joy of having a child. Children show the world to parents in a new, exciting way. The simple questions and deep interest of the child may surprise and challenge the parent to have another think about or take on situations that have not been considered for some time, perhaps not at all. Child and parent can share a mutual process in which they show the world to one another in a new, fresh way. The young child and the parent, and, sometimes, the grandparent, discover and rediscover the world with new eyes. And such exploration and experimentation can be enlivening and enriching. The young child marvels at the world and such joy can be shared with the parent. Nature provides some of these deep delights: for example, the excitement of touching the bark of a tree, the wonder of planting little seeds carefully, and waiting for them to grow, and then seeing them grow. These experiences form lasting memories.

At this age, children seem to use all their senses to relate to and absorb new aspects of their outside world. I have seen little children watching the rain fall and trying to catch a raindrop on their tongues or with their hands, or laughingly stretch out an arm or leg to touch a sunbeam. I have seen them run out to taste snow for the first time. I have observed them smelling a flower with some apprehension, and touching the bonnet of a car left in the summer sun to spring back when surprised by its heat. Children of this age like to repeat these experiences, often several times, thereby taking in these new discoveries and making them part of their own knowledge of the world around them.

Children of this age are moving with their minds just as they move their bodies to explore their world. They are finding their mental muscles and testing out how far their growing minds can stretch.

Thrills are waiting to be discovered in the bodily sensations of the two-, three-, four- and five-year-old who delights in hanging upside down just for the experience of it. The display of the body and physical contact can create much excitement and pleasure. Apart from the frequently heard laughter and screams which accompany chasing games, children of this age are both excited and stimulated by the discovery of what they can do with their bodies and their growing mastery of those bodies.

This is illustrated in the following two examples.

> Jennie (four years and four months old), Susie (four years and seven months old), and Carlo (four years and eight months old) have intertwined their legs into a group knot. Much giggling and excitement accompany their attempts to disentangle. Carlo laughs, exclaiming half-anxiously, half-excitedly, "I'm stuck, I'm stuck."

> Daisy (three years and nine months old) tells Tracey (three years and four months old), "Pull your mouth off." Tracey obliges in mime. Daisy giggles. This is repeated; both children laugh excitedly. Daisy says, "Pull your head off." Much laughter follows Tracey's actions. Then Daisy instructs, "Pull your body off." Both girls laugh wildly as Tracey wriggles and pulls at her clothes (Davids, 1987, p. 310).

For the nursery age child, the world is full of surprises and of skills waiting to be discovered. The discovery of each simple skill involves concentration, focus, and persistence. Through repetition, the newfound skills are gradually mastered. There then comes a point of celebration, at first perhaps with the adult, and then a more private sense of joy and celebration.

> Three-year-old Alex holds his Dad's hand while he painstakingly negotiates the descent of the steps, one by one, in the underground. His face is concentrated on lowering his left leg down on to the next step, and each time his dad counts the step. This is a feat for the young child and a feat that requires patience on the part of the adult who steadies the child and adds to his achievement by counting aloud; the little boy listens to the increasing numbers and to the tone of the father's voice. When he reaches the bottom of the stairs, Alex looks up into his father's face. They smile at one another.

Other important milestones are bladder and bowel control; since the toddler years, the child has gradually been moving out of his parent's taking care of his body to the state of being able to be in charge of his own body. The parent encourages her child's gradual independence by slowly relinquishing different aspects of the looking after and encouraging the child to do them for himself. For example, instead of the parent acting on the child's wriggling about as a sign of needing to use the toilet, the parent may point out the connection to the child and ask him whether he needs to use the toilet. The child may resent the interruption to his play. However, if the parent praises her child's attainment of these small steps, the child may feel pleased with himself as well as realizing that this is another way of gaining his parent's approval. The young child has to work on reading the signals of his own body and knowing when to go to the toilet rather than leaving things to the last minute. He has to learn how it feels uncomfortable and urgent to want to wee or make a poo as well as how good it can feel in his body to do so. Parents can help by putting these sensations and feelings into words for the child and showing that they understand such experiences. Children may want the parent in the toilet with them; others may want the parent to stand nearby and then call them in. Toileting seems to be largely established *with* the child knowing his parent is alongside him, that is, that his parent understands the emotional issues that accompany this developmental achievement. It is a collaboration between each parent and individual child. In time, the little child feels increasingly proud of being in charge of his own bodily functions, and therefore of his self.

Common difficulties at this age are retention of stools and bedwetting.

For the young child his bodily products, particularly his poo, are precious parts of him; after all, they were inside and therefore were his. Some children may hold on to their stools rather like treasure that they do not want to give away. Sometimes they complain that it hurts to poo. Other children may dread the toilet itself and may fear that they too will drop down the watery hole and disappear into the pipes which make funny gurgling sounds. Some children fear that if they let go of their poo, something else of them will fall out. The parent may need much patience to weather her child's refusals and resistance; it may be helpful to know that many fears, as described above, may underlie this behaviour, and that in time, with encouragement and perhaps with some further questions by the child, such fears are likely to disappear.

The learning child needs encouragement and admiration from his parent that he can let go and has let go of what the child may see as parts of himself. Some children point to their poos and demand admiration of the very products themselves. Children often stand tall, looking bashfully proud when a parent or teacher admires their poos. Some children insist on waving goodbye to their poos. Curiosity and fear again may follow as the child watches the toilet flush and sees part of what was once him disappear in the swirling water. Holding on may also produce sensations that the nursery child rather likes, or feels excited by. His parent may sense the power struggle that may develop, with her child holding on until he *feels* ready.

Bedwetting is quite common at this age. There are usually many causes for it, including physical factors that influence the development of the control of the bladder. Essentially, different children mature physically at different rates. If the bedwetting goes on after age five, it may be worthwhile consulting a paediatrician to investigate underlying medical reasons. Some children do not have the attitude to bedwetting that the parent might expect. Children may experience lying in their own wee as one little girl expressed it, "lovely, wet and warm". In her case, she seemed to be rediscovering and returning to the pleasures associated with younger children; she was progressing well in many other ways and this bedwetting may have been her way of still holding on to more infantile pleasures. She also seemed to desire her mother's taking care of her body rather like a baby. Her mother decided to spend a slightly longer time at bedtime with her and within a few weeks the bedwetting diminished. The little girl was observed to spend more time in water play by herself and with her friends around this time. She seemed to have found a more mature way of expressing her preoccupation with water through the pleasures of splashing and paddling.

Bedwetting may be accompanied by nightmares: children literally wetting themselves out of fear. Some children may show their anxieties by bedwetting in response to changes of routine and of place, which accompany holidays. Other, bigger transitions, such as moving house, may also result in periods of bedwetting.

The parent's response to the bedwetting is important. The parent needs to allow herself to acknowledge the spectrum of feelings engendered by discovering that her child is bedwetting. The child needs the parent to know that it is happening. The parent may think that the child is doing it deliberately, and feel manipulated. It is helpful to know that, at this age, it is unlikely that this is the case.

Parents may feel ashamed about their child's bedwetting and benefit from the genuine support of other parents.

> Alice, five years and four months old, woke up in the night to discover
> that she had wet her bed. Alice looked worried when she woke up. At
> breakfast, her adopted mother sensed this and asked her what was the
> matter. Alice looked away, saying nothing. When mother returned
> from taking Alice to school, she discovered that one sheet was missing
> off Alice's bed. It had been stuffed into her box of toys. Mother realized
> that Alice had wet the bed. That afternoon after school, mother told
> Alice what she had found. Mother said she would not be cross as she
> understood that Alice might be worried how she might react. Mother
> said that some children wet the bed when there was something making
> them unhappy. Alice stayed very quiet. The next time (a few days later)
> that she wet the bed, she told her mother that it had happened again.
> Mother had been noticing that Alice seemed rather sad and clingy, and
> that her attitude towards school had changed. Alice dawdled in the
> mornings and complained of stomach-aches, saying she wanted to stay
> home. She had not done this previously. Mother could get no further
> clues from Alice.
>
> Eventually, it emerged that school had changed for Alice in that her
> usual teacher had had to go on leave and had been replaced with a
> teacher whom Alice experienced as strict and as someone who did not
> show affection with physical gestures. Alice was afraid of this new
> different teacher; she had started to be on her best behaviour as if she
> were a guest in a new family. It emerged that she felt under pressure
> to be extra good and to please this teacher, who demanded more
> grown-up behaviour. Alice missed the teacher who was absent, partic-
> ularly her more informal manner and the times when she let Alice sit
> on her lap. Alice missed her physically demonstrative style.
>
> When this was put into words for her by her adoptive parents, Alice's
> behaviour changed a little. Mother had a talk with the new teacher who
> then made a special effort to praise Alice's efforts, and also showed
> Alice her interest in Alice's playfulness and capacity to imagine.
>
> The bedwetting seemed to be Alice's way of reacting to the loss of her
> trusted teacher and to the strain of her perceptions that she would not
> be able to live up to the expectations and earn the approval of the new
> teacher. The new teacher may have felt like another adoptive parent,
> with whom Alice felt she had to be on her best behaviour for fear of
> rejection. The fact that Alice had rather idealized her inconsistent

biological mother in the first two years of her life may well have contributed to her reaction to the sudden unexpected change in staff.

Mother acknowledged her own annoyance about the bedwetting, and some of her own disgust in finding the wet sheets. She was also aware of her feelings abut her lack of privacy, as Alice had followed her almost everywhere for a few weeks. Alice's clinging reminded her of a toddler. As Alice regained her confidence in school and began to develop a relationship with her teacher, the bedwetting diminished.

Interestingly, Alice tried to deal with her distress by creating a split in her behaviour. She felt compelled to be very good, strong at school with the new teacher. At home, however, the smaller, over-whelmed, anxious, and tearful aspects of herself were expressed in Alice's wetting the bed, dawdling, stomach-aches, and clinging.

Alice's experiences are complex. For many children, it is suffi-cient for parents to show that they are aware of the bedwetting or the messing and that they believe in the child's capacity to control his sphincters. As discussed earlier in this chapter, the parent can encourage her child's discovering and achieving such control by appropriate praise.

CHAPTER FOUR

Separation

Coping with separation is another crucial developmental achievement, and one that the nursery age child has been struggling towards and grappling with during the toddler years. The capacity to stand on one's own two feet has its foundations in the numerous experiences of closeness with mother. Separation is based on the feeling of being with another person, on togetherness. There is much in separation that is paradoxical, in that one can only be without the other by having enough of them inside one. After the early experiences of being loved and understood and having one's needs regularly read and met, young children learn to be alone in the presence of mother: for example, playing contentedly by themselves while mother is talking on the telephone, or unpacking the shopping, or preparing lunch. It is quite fascinating to see the child every now and again lifting his eyes and checking that his mother is still there: the intervals between checks get longer and longer as the child feels safe in the knowledge that his mother is now held inside him, in his mind.

During the toddler years, there is much toing and froing, with the child going off on excursions away from the parent to return to the safe base. The role of the parent is crucial in that he or she needs to be there, both physically and emotionally, in order for the child to leave him or her. The experiences of leaving and being left are profound and evoke strong feelings, and we revisit them throughout the life cycle when we confront changes both in our relationships and in our work.

Separation experiences are bound up with the kind and quality of the relationships that the young child has. The child who has a good enough relationship with the parent he fundamentally trusts will, in time, develop the capacity to bear the impatience which accompanies separation and will wait in confidence with the positive expectation that she will return. The child who experiences the parent as patchy or unreliable, or who has a troubled relationship, may be overcome by panic or anger at the absence. As the child matures, he can bring more of his own resources to manage the feelings stirred up by being left. The story of *Owl Babies* (Waddell & Benson, 1992) illustrates this poignantly as, in reaction to the mother owl's departure, the smallest of the three owls, can only say, "I want my mummy". The smallest owl is left with the raw feelings, like the younger child, as he does not yet have the ability of the older sibling owls to think about and comprehend what might have happened to his mum. The older siblings turn to the internal images or pictures of the mother in their minds.

Separation has different meanings at different ages. At worst, the child who is left feels that he has lost good feelings about himself: being left lowers his good feelings about himself, his self-esteem. The child in this scenario can feel not only abandoned by the loved person, but also bereft of the love of that person. He feels literally "out of sight, out of mind" in the eyes and heart of the treasured other on whom he is dependent.

Separation can, therefore, be associated with feelings of being abandoned or of being rejected for another, as in sibling rivalry, or in feeling left out by the parent enjoying the company of the other parent, or be associated with feeling betrayed, as with a new baby or with the preference for another relationship.

> I remember playing with a friend's three-year-old boy, David; we were getting on very well, with him showing me some of his toys and possessions, introducing me to the family dog, and asking me, in a manner reminiscent of someone working their way towards asking a

woman out for a date, whether I liked the video, *Beauty and the Beast*. I indicated that I would like to see it. It was time for lunch and we did not get to see the video. Some time later, when I was saying my good-byes, David looked up at me. His Dad asked him to say goodbye to me. He sat on the floor and grumpily mumbled, "I no like you no more." He refused to say goodbye and would not look at me.

This was at a time when David was struggling with his parents' recent separation, and perhaps, at the moment of my departure, I felt to him like his mother, who now lived in another house. Clearly, he felt he had not had enough time with me, that I had not watched his video, and he felt frustrated and angry with me.

Children may need help with their separation experiences when they enter nursery school. Many schools are well versed in facilitating this achievement, which is one constructed by both parent and child. I have seen many children struggling with their own feelings and experiences of separating, which is a task in and of its own right, and, in addition, being affected by the experiences of their parents. This can become too much of a burden for the child. For example, the child who feels a little anxious about leaving his mother needs a clear message from her that she *is* going and that she *will* be back and that she believes that he *can* manage this separation. If she dillydallies, she sends out a message that she is not sure whether he can cope, and this complicates matters for the child. Separating is something of a dance performed by mother and child—there has to be a mutual understanding, spoken and unspoken. The issue of separation brings with it the issue of two persons' needs, the parent and the child. Mother may wish to reclaim her own private needs. She has to allow herself to move away, as well as let her child move away. Powerful feelings in her, such as guilt and anger, may result in her cutting and running rather sharply. Yet, if she stays and frets at the point of the goodbye, she also communicates her anxieties, which may then augment her child's fears. Her child may sense her ambivalence about letting him go, and try to stop her from leaving.

The charming film, *Finding Nemo*, has separation as its main theme. Nemo is his father's only surviving son. Father Fish watches the exuberant Nemo closely; it is clear that having recently lost his wife, Nemo's mother, when Nemo was very small, Father Fish is worried about losing his son. His overprotective attitude is particularly apparent when he takes Nemo to his first day at school. Nemo defiantly rebels against his father's various warnings not to swim away. The film portrays vividly how a parent, especially a traumatized one, can struggle to give his child the space and freedom to explore. The child can begin to feel trapped and hampered and angrily break away in a manner that then only raises the parent's anxieties even more.

On the other hand, the child who has to wait for his mother to fetch him and is the last one to be collected may feel that her lateness is evidence of her not liking him. He may experience being kept waiting as evidence of not being valued enough. There has to be a credit of reliability, an accumulation of many good experiences before the child can hold on to the idea that mummy likes him even when she comes late to collect him.

Separations and their counterpart, reunions, are an inevitable part of life. They are often not comfortable, but the intense feelings that accompany them can be recognized, experienced, and, to some extent, managed and mastered by the young child with the help of his parents.

Different children deal with separation differently.

Three-and-a-half-year-old Max nestled close to his father, asking him to make a book with photographs of his dad. When his father asked why, the little boy said, "Because you might go away." His dad reassured him that this was not the case. Max repeated "Because you might go away", and then the father understood that he meant die. He said "I understand", and reassured his son that this was unlikely to happen. They bought a scrapbook and collected a few photographs together. The album did not get worked on much, as Max seemed to feel understood by his dad. This occurred at a time when his father worked late nights and his mother was rather preoccupied with her own worries.

Here, the child felt that his communication was received, responded to, and understood, although not immediately by his father. The boy got his message across, in fact showed a determination to do so. And the father responded and addressed his fears, reassuring him. The feeling of being understood seemed to override the need for the photographs that would have served as a literal reminder of the father–son relationship.

For some children like Max, separation means gone forever, no return: that is, death. It can take some time to learn from one's own experiences that when parents are absent, they have not necessarily gone for ever.

> This same little boy used his imagination to help him manage his lone-liness. There were no similar age children in the neighbourhood and he often sensed his mother's emotional unavailability. He imagined that he had three imaginary friends Old Brixton, Chummy, and Brer. His father worked in Brixton at the time; Chummy was rather like the boy himself, a kind of friendly twin, and Brer was from the Brer Rabbit books that his father used to read him. The boy creatively kept the pres-ence of his father and activities he enjoyed with his father in his heart and mind through his imaginary companions. (See Chapter Eight, "The imaginary and the real".)

Parents cannot be present 100 per cent of the time; however, there are times when the parent may be preoccupied or worried and, therefore, cannot hold the child in the front of their minds. The parent disconnects from the child; for the moment the connection between them is lost. At such times the child may sense the parent's mind being elsewhere, and one possible response is to get lost oneself. Anna Freud (1967) describes a little boy lost in a large department store who, after being reunited with his mother, accused her tearfully, "You losted me", thereby expressing his feel-ings that she had neglected him.

She also writes about children who have been separated from their parents, for example, evacuated at the time of war, not only having to manage their own distress but also the imagined distress of the parent left behind. "I must telephone my mummy, she will be so lonely" was a common response of young children, especially at the end of the day. Nursery school children often ask their teacher after a weekend or holiday what she has done "all alone", whether she has "missed" them. Sometimes, the children attempt to cope with their own feelings of loneliness and yearning to be in touch by shifting the painful longings into the people to whom they are attached.

Yet, separations are an inevitable part of life; the pain, fears, and uncomfortable feelings that accompany them can be lived through and overcome by parent and child. Not all children respond with the same degree of upset.

Four-year-old Matthew had been left by his dad for a short while at a family friend's house. He sat on the floor and was drawing. After about ten minutes he heard sounds from outside, stopped drawing, and asked, "Daddy's car?" The family friend checked and said, "No not yet." Matthew went back to his drawing, then he left it aside and looked a little dreamy. The family friend offered him a drink and he nestled close to her while drinking it slowly. There were sounds again from the street. The doorbell rang and Matthew ran to hug his dad, who smiled at him. When his dad picked him up, Matthew looked sleepy and sucked his thumb.

Matthew used his resources to cope with this separation; it was hard to wait for his dad, whom he expected to return. The presence of the friend helped him feel safe and comforted.

CHAPTER FIVE

Sleep and its complexities

A good night's sleep is not achieved once and for all. Sleep can be affected by the ongoing preoccupations of the young child. There are many issues that may contribute to sleeping difficulties at this time of life. Anxieties around separation, concerns about the child's relationships with his parents or with his siblings, as well as dilemmas in expressing strong feelings, may all show in sleeping problems. Ideas stirred up by watching television, or by witnessing an unusual event in the day, or by encountering something puzzling and new by which the child feels touched, can all affect sleep and cause temporary problems. Sometimes, the parent can help her child by listening for and talking about what has stayed with him, and by trying to put the worrying bit that is preoccupying and/or exciting for the child, literally buzzing around his head, in a kind of perspective. For example,

> Four-and-a-half-year-old Tommy said he could not sleep because of the hammer. His mother remembered that he had visited the doctor a few days before. He had fallen, and, as part of the examination, the doctor had tested his reflexes with a hammer. At the time, Tommy had showed no particular reaction. His mother asked whether there was

something about the hammer that he did not like. He replied that the hammer made his body jump and that felt funny. Slowly, he and his mother worked out that Tommy was worried that his body could suddenly start to jump or go wobbly again. He was much relieved when his mum explained what the doctor had been doing and why he had done it. It seemed that Tommy was anxious that he, after his fall, was losing control of his ability to move and stop his body.

There may be battles around the act of being told that it is time for bed. The child may experience this as an interruption to his play, a cutting across his pleasure. At times like this, his parent may feel like a meany. The anger and sense of injustice with the parent may be expressed by comparisons with the siblings. The familiar protest about older sisters and brothers being allowed to stay up later may indicate the feelings about being in a certain position in the family, with its relative freedoms and restrictions.

The extra time given by the parents to an older sibling may attract feelings of injustice and jealousy. Being grown-up is simply equated with staying up later, rather like the marks made on the wall indicating the changing height of the growing child. It may be hard for the parent to stand by the rule, as she may come to feel that she is being overly strict, spoiling her child's fun, and even taking sides with the older children's rights. It is crucial that the parent does not simply confirm her child's interpretation of "parental injustice": giving in to her child may be perceived by the child as an admission of having been unfair.

Allied difficulties are the frequent struggles around staying settled in bed. The child may resent the rule that he has to remain settled while others are still awake and together; the child may rebel against a sense of missing out. Underneath the protest, and what can develop into a power struggle, may lurk the child's passionate feelings of exclusion from the parents' relationship. After all, to the young child's mind, the parents sleep together in one bed, whereas the child sleeps alone in a single bed. The various calls for a glass of water, for the door to be opened more, or about an imaginary spider, may be the child's fearing aloneness or his attempt to separate the parents. Equally, the child may make use, knowingly or half-knowingly, of these night-time needs, complaints, and upsets to engage in a game of musical beds, with Mum coming to share a bed while Dad sleeps alone, or vice versa. If this becomes a frequent occurrence, the child can feel a sense of power and triumph that may not be helpful to his ongoing development, nor helpful in accepting his position in the family and in managing to cope with the painful feelings of exclusion. The parent who conveys that she will do anything for some sleep and who, albeit with irritation, allows the child to take his dad's place in the parental bed, is communicating a message to the child that he can get close to her and get dad out of the way. If the parent marks the territory and the time firmly, the message is different—perhaps saying, "I'll come to stay near you for a little while until you fall asleep and then I am coming back to my bed". This might not work the first few times, but, as the child realizes that his parent is not at his beck and call at any minute of the night, and that the parent genuinely believes that he can settle in his own bed and go to sleep, such problems may gradually disappear. The parent may need to consider whether there is any possible reason why she might not be able to set limits. Is there some comfort in having her daughter sleep in her bed when dad is away on business trips? Has her daughter picked up her mother's unacknowledged need for close company?

Sleep difficulties may be associated with ongoing struggles with separation.

Sleep may be experienced as a time when the child struggles to withdraw, not only into sleep, but away from his relationship with the parent. Darkness can be perceived by the child as all-consuming, overwhelming, unknown, and frightening, inducing a state of helplessness and being alone with fear. Some children, struggling with separation issues, may experience the darkened room and state of being alone as dangerous and terrifying, and need to turn to loved people to provide protection.

Sigmund Freud describes the dilemma of a three-year-old boy in a moving footnote. The little boy was calling out of a dark room where he was sleeping:

> "Auntie, speak to me! I'm frightened because it's so dark." His aunt answered him: "What good would that do? You can't see me." "That doesn't matter," replied the child, "if anyone speaks, it gets light." [Freud, 1905d, p. 224]

The boy pinpoints how the sound of her voice, the sense of being connected to her and reassured by her presence, diminishes his fears of and about the dark.

The aunt adopts a rather rational, logical approach, and the articulate boy shows her how he is held by her voice, how hearing her provides him with safety and comfort, making all the difference in helping him handle his fearfulness.

A similar theme runs through the book *Can't You Sleep, Little Bear?* (Waddell & Firth, 1988); the little bear cannot fall asleep because he is scared of "the dark all around us". The big bear tries various practical solutions, including providing a series of bigger and brighter lights. It is only when the big bear takes the little bear outside, where they look at the dark together and find the moon and the stars, that the little bear falls asleep and remains asleep in the big bear's arms. Similar to the boy above, it seems to be the comforting presence of the parent that diminishes anxieties and enables the transition to sleep. With the recurrence of such comforting experiences, the child gradually takes in enough of this consoling presence, which then allows him to find enough inner strength to face the dark alone.

Parents often develop bedtime rituals that are familiar to the child, providing a known experience that eases the transition into sleeping alone. Sometimes, parent and child talk about the events of the day, remembering the details and sequences; this may be an opportunity to digest new experiences. They may also talk about the plans for the following day. Sometimes, the parent sings a song, or tells or reads a story as part of this transition from wakefulness to sleep. When the parent sings or reads a story, it is not only the content, but also the sound of her voice, together with the words and looking at the pictures, that evoke safety and sleep. The young child may ask for a repetition of a particular type of a story or that story again—this may contribute to the atmosphere of familiarity. For example, the book *Guess How Much I Love You* (McBratney & Jeram, 1994), is a charming tale of how Little Nutbrown Hare and Big Nutbrown Hare describe how much they love one another. The upshot is that little Nutbrown Hare, who is reluctant to withdraw into sleep, falls asleep, feeling treasured and loved. This reassurance of love may ease the passage into sleep and the transitory separation from the child's everyday world and his parents. The child's favourite cuddly toys may offer him some consolation with this transition. The child relies on the presence of the special toy to help carry him through the sense of aloneness as he literally lets go of his parents and his hold on his daytime world, and enters the world of sleep. It is important that the parent respects the child's need for this cuddly presence to remain the same, and not change it by washing it or replacing it without the child's knowledge. In time, when the child has grown more confident and is ready, these possessions will not be relied on or needed with the same intensity.

Not every child and parent have such bedtime rituals. Indeed, some children might not need such help with this nightly transition. The absence of a ritual is not a sign of disturbance or a sign of cruelty. The parent may have made an accurate assessment of what that particular child needs. Regular behaviour may provide a comforting security to the child.

Night-time fears are common at this age. The pre-school child's imagination is fertile and, at the end of a busy day in the silence of the bedroom, preoccupations can take and find shape, sometimes of large proportions. Such fears are vivid and real to the child, and cannot easily be dispelled by adults' reasoning. For the young child, the night-time lion who is hiding in the cupboard is real in his mind, as real as if the lion were standing there. (See Chapter Eight on the Imaginary and the Real.) To a child, familiar objects in the bedroom can look very different in the dark. Familiar things can become fearsome: for example, the well-known pattern on the curtains can suddenly resemble nasty pirates, sinister dragons, or gobbling giants.

These imaginings may be understood as linked to the child's close relationships. The nasty pirates may be embodiments of the child's own competitive feelings and wishes to steal the parents' attention away from younger siblings. The lion in the cupboard may be associated with the child's anger and wish to take over the parent's position of power. There may be hidden wishes to displace Daddy, and be Mummy's number one, together with the fear of reprisal for such wishes.

From the parents' point of view, they can see the child's panic and terror, but not all children are able to put into words what exactly is creating their sense of dread. It is even possible that, paradoxically, the parent trying to reassure the child happens to be precisely the person that the child is afraid of, and when the child rejects that parent's approach and shows an increased sense of panic, we have a parent who feels at a loss as to how to proceed. That is why, from a practical point of view, it may be best to comfort the child without making any attempt to reassure him, unless and until the child is able to articulate what specifically is giving rise to his fears. When this happens, instead of simply trying to convince the child that there is no reason for his anxiety, it is best to help him to explain how the particular fear came into being. This is easier said than done, but it is still an effort worth making, since the child's "explanation / investigation" will bring more effective and lasting relief than any words from the parents.

Still from a practical point of view, it is important to keep the child in his bed, and if the child wants to go somewhere else, then some "neutral" place should be chosen. We know only too well that the easiest way of dealing with these nightmares or panic attacks is to invite the child to sleep in the parents' bed, but this contains the serious danger of setting off a pattern where the child may unconsciously long to find a special place in the parents' bed.

Children begin to recall their dreams at this age. Sometimes when they wake from a frightening dream, they remain confused, and not able to make the distinction between the witch or wizard of their dream and the real parent who comes to find out what is wrong. Some children cannot let go of the world of the imagination so easily; it is as if they get stuck or trapped in the nightmare or dream world, or they take time and may need help to clarify their confusion between the two worlds of reality and dream. They may need support from the parent to manage a sense of disappointment that the magic of the dream is not to be found in reality: the wished-for dream doll or dream bike is only imaginary. Indeed, sometimes children can feel relief that the dream dangers are not real.

Less troublesome sleeping difficulties may occur when the child's usual pattern is disrupted by external changes, for example, sleeping in a strange environment at holiday time. Excitement and anxiety about the unknown may contribute to the experiences of being unsettled.

Changes in the family may interrupt sleep, and the child's perception of his mother's pregnancy or his father's increased absences from home may constitute a new set of worries and cause inner instability.

> Three-year-old Mark woke his mother with frequent stomach upsets in the first few months after the birth of his baby brother, thereby asserting his own need for care and attention. He seemed to be communicating his jealousy of his mother feeding his new brother at night.

It can be helpful for parents and children to address these messages in the day. This boy's mother made a special time each day to spend solely with him, doing activities he chose. She also talked to him about how hurt he was and how jealous he felt of his little brother, especially when he knew they were together on their own. She emphasized that she loved him just the same as before this new baby came along. Some children may feel that their whole world has been realigned and changed by the presence of a sibling, and need many reassurances by their parents of the stability and continuity of their parents' love. There is much to be said for telling the child that he is now older and therefore has different needs and abilities. The parent's reassurance and firmness are equally important: consistency always reassures the child.

CHAPTER SIX

Additions: relationships with siblings

Much has been written on the subject of sibling rivalry. The child's world undergoes a massive change; indeed, for some children, it can feel as if the world has turned upside down and will never be the right way up again when they realize that there is to be an addition to the family. Of course, the hardest part of it is that children have no choice in the matter; they may experience the pregnancy of the mother and her preoccupation as a betrayal and as confirmation that they were not good or sufficient. The new baby can be perceived as endangering what seemed to be a settled and safe relationship to mother and father. The nub of the fear seems to lie in the child's anxieties that his connection to his mum and dad will change or be lost. The task that faces him is his need to discover and, indeed, re-discover that his own unique place in the hearts of his parents can be maintained and even continue to grow. The child comes to learn this through experiences, not only by being told and reassured. The new baby can be felt as threatening and lead to feelings of dislike and even hatred, as well as curiosity and pride and love. The news of this momentous change in family life is likely to be met with mixed feelings by the young child. In time, the negative and uncomfortable feelings can be accepted and worked on by the child and his parents, and lead to more affectionate feelings.

First the child reacts to the news of mother's pregnancy; some children may withdraw or regress (that is, act like a younger child), becoming more dependent, almost as if they were saying, "I am still a baby too. I need your attention." Other children may act as if nothing has happened, yet be listening out acutely for information and watching for changes in mummy, such as her changing shape, the food she eats, her mood. Others may ask many questions as a way of dealing with this change in the family and in their worlds. Alongside taking in the surprise of this tumultuous news begins the process of making sense of how it had happened. The curious child also begins to think about some of the most profound questions. Where do babies come from? How was the baby made? And, of course, such interest in origins and conception is bound up with how he, the child, began. Many children are actively pondering and puzzling over these questions, and parents may be surprised by the freshness and inventiveness of the child's own explanations.

To return to the reactions about the newcomer. Children of this age indicate their wish that the new baby is a temporary visitor, rather than someone here to stay, by asking when the baby is going back to the shop or the hospital, rather like a book on loan from the library. It is as if the child's tolerance for the newcomer has gone past his inwardly set expiry date. Young children often wish the baby away, or, on its arrival, show their impulse to get rid of the rival by, for example, assigning the baby to the dustbin.

Some children react by increased calls for attention to parents and visitors that seem to highlight the message, "Don't forget about me. I am here too!"

> Five-year-old Nick lay down next to the Moses basket which contained his sleeping baby brother and, stretching to his full length, said to me, "Look how much bigger I am."

Nick seemed to be attempting to find another role for himself as the big one, referring literally to his body and asserting himself. It is the big feelings, which include jealousy and exclusion, that children are struggling to master.

For some children the idea of their parents having another child is experienced as an outrage: "They have got me—why do they want anyone else?" The child can feel very wounded by the sense of being ousted, of no longer being the sole object of attention. Some children have told me that they felt there was something wrong with them and this was the reason their parents needed to make another baby.

Much attention has been focused on the subject of sibling rivalry, which is, of course, an important issue for the growing child. What has received less attention is the positive side of relationships between sisters and brothers. In recent years (Provence & Solnit, 1983; Mitchell, 2003; Coles, 2006) more notice has been given to the value of the sibling relationship. Children themselves have voiced their valuing of their siblings. Some children have powerful wishes for a younger playmate, for example: someone to dress up or play with? They might also wish for someone smaller whom they can influence and treat in ways that they were treated by the parents. The younger sibling can view his older sibling as a model, someone to emulate. Often the language development of younger siblings proceeds faster. The younger sibling may be stimulated by the speech and play of his older brothers and sisters. The older sibling may be regarded by the younger child as a source of comfort or as a protector, as someone who can understand what it is like to be struggling with conflicts and passions that are not far removed from the older child's experience. Younger children may seek older sisters and brothers as allies, to deal with other children, or sometimes in protest against the demands of their parents.

It is as if many nursery age children possess a template for the concept of family. And, mostly, family means having more than one child.

> As five-year-old Betty announced emphatically to her parents when her baby brother arrived, "Now, we are a proper family."

Sometimes it is easier, contrary to expectation, for the child to tolerate the idea of having someone of the same gender, a smaller version of themselves who they can encourage, correct, and be admired by. This idea is captured well in Tony Ross's book *I Want a Sister* (Ross, 2001). The Little Princess's reaction to the news of the new baby is one of delight in that she wants a sister, someone like her. She has to come to terms with her dislike of brothers and her wish to cancel out any similarity between boys and girls. For some children, the fear is that someone of a different gender will ruin their own special place in the family.

> Five-year-old Jason wanted a little brother who "I can play with . . . He'll be better than Sally [his older sister] . . . we can play boys' things . . . football . . . He can have my clothes that are small for me."

It may well be that this little boy's wish for a little brother play-mate is his way of dealing with his older sister, whom he experienced as bossy.

The idea of an addition to the family may stimulate the child's curiosity and thinking about reproduction and how babies are made. Children may become aware of the parent's preoccupation and of their changed behaviour. This is illustrated in a group of young children aged four to six, commenting on one of the children's pregnant mother: "She spends so much time in the loo. Why doesn't she call the new baby Lou?"

It may well be that their own wishes to get rid of the new baby as well as their anger about the mother's attention being elsewhere contributed to their remark.

There may also be strong wishes to communicate directly with the growing addition.

> Four-year-old Lizzie showed her wish to talk to the baby living inside her mother. One day she was in the bath with her pregnant Mum. "Open your mouth, I want to speak to the baby."

One is struck by her sense of the close connection of the baby to her mum, and the idea that she can send a message directly through her mum's mouth to the baby. The baby has a real presence inside her mother's body and the four-year-old Lizzie attempts to make a relationship with this person.

> Three-year-old Matthew seemed to be trying to figure out how his mother had a baby inside her. He asked his pregnant mother, "Where did you get the baby from? She answered, " From Daddy." Later that day, when playing with his Dad, Matthew said " Dad, I've got to tell you . . . The baby you gave Mummy . . . she ate it."

In his mind, it seems that his mother had swallowed her husband's gift as one might eat tasty chocolates; this three-year-old boy has the idea that the baby is inside his mother and has constructed an explanation of how the baby got in there and why his mother's body is fat. The literal interpretation of the father's gift to the mother contains a child-like logic. What is inside has been taken in from outside through the mouth.

Children are often weaving their own theories about how babies are made, extrapolating from their observations and from their imagination. It can be helpful for the parent to respond by listening to and following the logic of these theories. In time, usually in response to her child's spontaneous questions and curiosity, the parent can explain the facts.

There is an amusing book by Babette Cole, called *Mummy Laid an Egg* (1993), which contains a reversal of the usual state of affairs. The parents are full of fanciful ideas about the facts of life, which they share by way of informing their son and daughter. The children laugh at their ideas and point out the parts of their explanations that are correct. The children then proceed to put the parents right by teaching them, using a series of anatomical and stick figure drawings, explaining in detail how parents join together in sex to make babies.

The message I am trying to convey is that "additions" is an alive topic that may generate embarrassment, anxiety, and a curious mixture of fantasy and fact. Children may be helped to express their ideas in this regard; parents may struggle to talk about this subject in a straightforward manner. They may have to revisit how this was handled in their families of origin, and rethink their ways of responding to their children's questions and thinking. It is important for parents to bear in mind their child's capacity to understand all the new information. Difficulties can arise when the parent overestimates her child's ability to comprehend.

Parents play an important part in helping the relationship between the siblings take shape. The parent may help her older child to recognize and bear his strong feelings towards his little sibling. When his mother makes sense of why his baby sister is crying, he can begin to reflect on his own reaction, and develop a sense of what causes his sister's behaviour. Such understanding opens up the ways in which he might chose to respond.

The parent may need to act as a kind of mediator and protector of her different aged children with their differing developmental needs. The nursery age child may be happily engrossed in using the blocks to build a castle. His toddler brother may watch this construction and then, following his own needs, stretch out to knock the towers down. The older sibling may feel annoyed and frustrated. The parent may help by explaining to the older child that this is what his toddler sibling likes to do, and by creating a separate space where this can happen. She might suggest to the older child that he build elsewhere, higher up beyond the reach of his brother. She might also talk to the young toddler, warning him to leave alone his older sibling's castle, as well as give the toddler more opportunities to build and then knock his own constructions down. In this way she protects both children's development and interests.

It is likely that there will be times when it all becomes too much for the older child to bear. He may push the toddler off balance when he is pulling himself up; he may lose patience with him and grab back the toy he has taken. The parent may have to tolerate a certain amount of this behaviour and perhaps respond to the backsliding of her older child with sympathy; each parent has to decide at what point they draw the line. It is very hard for many nursery age children to be the big one all the time; the parent's acknowledgement of this struggle and of the conflict between the wish to be the big one and the wish to behave like a little child again may contribute to the child's feeling that he is understood and felt for. There are also likely to be times when the parent feels that both children are asking too much, and that she herself feels close to the end of her tether. At such times, she may need to turn to support, of her partner, of other mothers, or others who help her with the childcare.

Nursery age children can also show much tenderness towards their baby and toddler siblings. This can be something they have taken in from their parents.

Sam, three years and ten months old, solicitously picked up little beads from the kitchen floor. He came over to show them to his aunt, saying that they were too little and his baby sister might swallow them. His aunt praised him for his thoughtfulness.

Winnicott (1964) holds the view that children have children by proxy when their parents have them. A sibling can bring out maternal or paternal feelings in the little child and this is often seen in their play.

> A five-year-old little girl made use of her maternal feelings and her concern to help her little brother and her mother. Her toddler brother was screaming very loudly, piercing screams that were turning people's heads. She was holding a small glass bottle containing her food and watching him carefully. He was refusing the food his mother was trying to feed him. The little girl continued to watch him and she began to look distressed. She finished the food in her little pot and showed the empty bottle to her mum, who indicated a bin where she could dispose of it. Her brother carried on screaming and kicking out. She did not seem to know what to do and her mother seemed to be becoming somewhat exasperated. Her mother gave her the pot from which she had been trying to feed her brother, addressing her affectionately as her darling. The little boy began to watch his sister as she started to eat from the pot. He was quiet for a brief moment and then began to screech again. His sister stood there watching him and after a little while, she asked him whether he wanted some; he gestured, indicating it seemed, his interest. Then, solicitously, she fed him from the pot one spoonful at a time. He calmed, as did her mother. The little girl indicated when the pot was empty and her mother looked pleased. All three were then silent. It seemed that a little crisis had been negotiated.

This situation contains many aspects about which one might entertain several views. The five-year-old girl shows her capacity to identify with her unhappy brother and with her mother. When the little boy sees his food being eaten by his sister, and becomes aware of his mother's affection to his litle sister, he changes his mind and wants the food and, perhaps, what his sister shares with his mother. His sister then adopts the role of her mother and feeds him. Mother, perhaps intuitively aware of her son's desires, allows her daughter to step into her role and give her brother some of what he feels to be his share of mother.

One common way of coping with the addition who is here to stay is to imagine that one has one's own baby to look after, thereby "becoming" the parent and developing the maternal or paternal feelings that Winnicott (1964) has described. One frequently sees mothers wheeling buggies alongside their daughters proudly pushing their own miniature buggies containing well looked after baby dolls. This kind of meaningful play can underlie the reality of becoming a mother later in adult life.

CHAPTER SEVEN

Words and thinking

I t has been apparent in the preceding chapters that children's minds are very much at work on puzzling out their experience of the people and world around them. The words the nursery age child is beginning to use reveal the quality and depth of his thinking. The child's play with toys is accompanied by play with ideas, which are expressed in experimenting with communicating by talking. The parent can find her child's new capacities exciting. She may feel relieved that communication with her maturing child relies less on inference than during the toddler years. She may come to realize how such new developments also require patience and an ability to tolerate puzzlement on her part.

Some children start to "join in the conversation", frequently prompted by the wish to speak as their siblings do. It is not unusual for a younger child to speak at a younger age than his older brother or sister did. Siblings may encourage the younger child to use words, and spur on his development. The young child may need help from siblings and parents to clarify what he is saying and to gently correct him.

The path to speech is not always smooth. Children may go through a time when they stutter. There are many reasons why a young child may stutter, but the most common cause at this age seems to be a mixture of excitement, anxiety, and self-conscious-ness. The child may be in a rush to get out the words that carry his perceptions and thoughts and, in this flutter, stumble and stutter over the sounds. At this age, the child may sense a different quality of attention, and perhaps expectation, which may serve to make him self-conscious that he is indeed speaking and being listened to. The parent of the stuttering child can help her child by giving him a message to take his time, and conveying that it is all right to stum-ble and get into muddles. Stuttering can cause alarm in the parent, generating feelings of impatience, frustration, and helplessness. It can be very hard not to talk for the child, guessing what he means. The stammering child can feel that his efforts have been in vain when his parent says the exact word he has been struggling, indeed fighting, to get out. Difficulties can arise if the child feels that his words have been taken from him; he may feel "Who is in charge here?" When the parent wonders alongside her child, the talking may then feel more like a joint effort rather than a potential battle. Stuttering usually subsides as the child grows more confident and relaxed. If, however, the stuttering continues and is causing the child distress, or the parent notices that the child is reluctant to speak, it might be worth discussing the situation with the nursery school teacher and even considering a referral for an assessment by a speech therapist.

The preschool child is developing language at speed now. For some time he has understood language more than he himself could use it. Now, with the encouragement and stimulation of adults, siblings, and other children, his language burgeons. There is a thrill in discovering words and playing with and mastering sounds. Children often find some words and expressions amusing, as they make them think of parts of their bodies or bodily activities.

Nursery age children are still very much involved in the mastery of toileting under the supervision of adults. Some of their preoccupations are evident in their laughter as in the following three examples:

> Susie (four years and two months old) and Jennie (four years old) are playing on the see-saw. Susie starts to chant "wee-wee, poo-poo" in rhythm with the rocking movement. They laugh with much pleasure (Davids, 1987, p. 309).

Mrs Z is cross with Daisy (three years and two months old). At story-reading time she warns the child, "If you carry on like that, you'll drive me potty." The group finds this very funny and there are roars of laughter.

Daddy is washing his hair; his twin girls, aged three, are watching him. Naomi asks, "Why are you glueing your head?" Her dad answers, "This isn't glue. It is special hair soap called shampoo." Lily says, "Nah! Poo is for bums!"

Words and things are still very close to one another in the preschool child's mind. Young children often construe words in a rather literal manner as in the example of the shampoo, where the sound "poo" was linked immediately to a specific part of the body, "bums".

Unfamiliar words may be heard as familiar sounds and given a different meaning by the child.

Henry, who was three years and ten months old, was standing next to the toilet, asking, "You're in?" He did this before he used the toilet and after he flushed it, watching the moving water with much concentration. His mother asked him what was happening. At first Henry did not answer. One day he said, "He lives in there", pointing to the toilet. It emerged that Henry believed in a fantasy monster who lived in the toilet. He believed this monster to be friendly and not likely to harm him. Henry said, "You talk to him too. I heard you." Henry's mother realized that she and her husband had used the word "urine" when talking in the bathroom. Gradually, the parents pieced together with Henry what had happened. Henry had overheard their conversation and understood "urine", an unknown word, to be "you're in". Henry had also heard his parents calling outside the the bathroom door, " Are you in?" He had then created a fantasy around the toilet and the water, which included an idea of a monster who lived in the toilet. Calling "You're in" was his way of addressing the monster.

Children start to play with words and use the play to express their feelings, as in the children who were angry about their pregnant mother spending so much time in the loo that they suggested she call the baby Lou. The name seemed to embody their jealousy over her preoccupation with her pregnancy and their desire to denigrate the newcomer.

The discovery of language at this age seems to be linked to bodily experiences, as if there is a pleasure in words which adds to the experience and captures the thrills and sensations of the bodily pleasure. This is illustrated in the following observation, where the pleasure in playing with rhyming words is combined with the thrill of bodily movement and excitement.

> Out of the blue, Susie (four years and two months old) sings out rather loudly, "not funny Bugs Bunny." She repeats this a number of times, smiling to herself as she moves among her peers in the garden. Jennie and Adele (both four years old) are playing with hula hoops. They begin to chant, "not funny Bugs Bunny" as they whirl their hoops around them. Their cries, interspersed with laughter, grow louder and louder the more excited they become. This game ends when the two girls become breathless from the combination of the chant, the whirling of their bodies, and their laughter (Davids, 1987, p. 309).

Young children have antennae; their grasp of language and their limited vocabulary perhaps heightens their sensitivity and emotional closeness to phenomena from which older children can maintain more of a distance.

They need time to process their reactions and can benefit from help from another person, such as a parent, teacher, or sibling to sort out their confusions. Words and things are still very close to one another in the preschool child's mind, as is particularly apparent in the following example:

> A family were holidaying at a seaside resort. One day the children noticed people gathering on the beach; they ran to investigate to find a porpoise that had been washed up. The porpoise was lying very still; some adults removed the seaweed from the porpoise's body and checked to see if the sea creature would move. The porpoise did not and the crowd agreed that it was dead. Five-year-old Tammy and her siblings touched and stroked the porpoise gently, remarking on the smooth quality of its skin. The children then carried on their swimming and other beach activities. At lunch at their holiday house that day, the mother offered Tammy some fruit salad. Tammy refused and looked a little worried. Her mother wondered why as Tammy was usually rather partial to fruit salad. She asked her what made her say no. Tammy said she did not want to eat porpoise. Her mother realized that she had said that the salad contained paw-paw today.

The similarity in sound between the two words evoked anxiety in Tammy, who did not want to eat a dead creature. She was still preoccupied with the dead porpoise, and her mother found her drawing the porpoise later in the day. During the following few days, Tammy asked questions about how the porpoise might have been hurt and about what would happen to the porpoise.

Children of this age use language to create language: for example, they make up their own words usually connected to the novel experiences. They experiment with words, like loo and Lou, described previously, and can be amazingly creative.

In previous chapters, we have looked at children's thinking about separation, conception, and birth. The concepts of death and loss are difficult phenomena for the young child to comprehend. Parents often want to shield their children completely from such experiences. This may not be possible, and the parent can play a key part in helping the child share their thoughts and feelings. The child may feel bewildered by his emotional experiences and by the tangle of his ideas and thoughts. Sometimes, children get a rather simple fix on an idea and need help from a parent to clarify and expand their thinking. Apparently nonsensical words or expressions should not be ignored or merely corrected. When the parent explores their meaning with the child, this may lead to the discovery of the ideas, sometimes quite amazing, underlying these creations. Parents are often surprised by how much thinking is going on in nursery age children's busy minds.

Frequently, nursery aged children form quick, passionate attachments to animals or children. Cuddly toys can bear significance way beyond the parent's imagination. The child is confronting, often for the first time the experiences of loss and death. And children's actions show their urgent desires; actions have to take the place of words that they have not found yet, or are on the way to finding. Their actions and play often show how much they are thinking about their experiences, as in the following example.

Four-and-a-half-year-old Robbie had a white mouse that died one day. The little boy dearly loved his pet. His father found him trying to push the dead mouse into the slot of his money box. This box looked like a metal trunk. When his father asked why he was doing this, the little boy said that he was posting his beloved mouse to God.

For nursery age children, concepts such as God or heaven have a concrete, nearby, immediate quality.

> Five-year-old Melanie shared her conviction with me that her uncle, who had recently died, could be found in her mother's friend's house. When I asked what made her think this, she said, "'Cos Mandy makes angel's delight . . . it's lovely." For her, heaven was just around the corner; in her mind, heaven was a place with angels and a place where sweet puddings called Angel's Delight were eaten.

Young children struggle to grasp the finality of death and what such an absence entails.

> For example, four-year-old Daniel, who lived in a distant continent from his grandmother, who had died a few months before, asked his parents, "Is Granny's house still there?" It was as if he was wondering whether his Granny's house had disappeared along with her, as if he was puzzled and beginning to distinguish between who and what dies, and what and who remains in place.

For some young children at this age, there is a permeability between fantasy and fact, between the concrete and the abstract, the real and the symbolic. Pretend and real are not so sharply differentiated. Parents may need to step in sometimes to make distinctions and show differences, and thereby help with the child's confusion between the literal and the figurative.

This is illustrated in the following example.

> Megan and Rosie, identical twins aged three years and eight months, rang the nursery school doorbell many times. When the teacher opened the door, she said jokingly, "Hold your horses." Rosie entered the nursery and the teacher looked around for Megan. She was still outside the nursery, carefully tying up her imaginary horses.

In Megan's play she has blurred the distinction between the imaginary and the real, and is engrossed in the world of pretend.

> While playing with a friend Tracey (four years and nine months old), five-year-old Annie noticed her gran's crosses and said, "My uncle wears one of those. He supports Manchester United." Tracey replied, very haughtily, "Don't be silly! You don't wear one of those if you support a football team. You wear one of those if you support Jesus."

Children's thinking can be quite amusing. Annie is making sense of what she sees; her friend's earnest correction is a little self-righteous. Tracey attributes a rather specific, literal view of the cross, namely that cross pertains only to Jesus. Both children have not reached a broader perspective of thinking, which involves entertaining the idea that symbols can belong to various ideas.

Often, children's attempts to understand lead to unusual connections and associations that can be creative and clear, and sometimes their comprehension and thinking can result in further muddles. An explanation can be woven around a word or a single fact; the child may be unwilling to let go of his theory or have someone question it. The personal explanation provides a sense of safety and "I-know-why", which the child is proud of and which may shield him from anxieties. Children of this age are often intrigued by other children's thinking. One sees this in story-creating by groups of children. One child may start to make a story by creating a character, for example, Bobby, who runs away from home. Other children may then join in the story-making, giving reasons why Bobby is running away and then offering to be another character, for example, his sister. The story can follow different directions and turns in plot, depending on the children's imaginations.

Paley (2004), an educationalist, describes many examples of small groups of nursery age children spontaneously creating stories together. They assign one another roles and the stories unfold as their ideas flow. Such dramatic play stimulates language and creates strong bonds between children. Some of these creations, described by Paley, appeared to be attempts by the children to make sense of dramatic events such as 9/11, when two aeroplanes were flown into the towers of the World Trade Centre in New York City, resulting in the deaths of many civilians.

As adults, we are often surprised by the depth of thinking and creativity in children's ideas. Winnicott writes of a strikingly precocious young girl,

Mary aged 2 years and 8 months had her friend Bridget to tea. Afterwards she said: "Mummy, I want Bridget's mind." What do you mean, dear?"—"I mean I want what she thinks with; so I'll be Bridget and Bridget'll be me." [Winnicott, 1936, pp. 60–61]

Some children seem to possess the capacity to stand outside themselves and view the passing of time, as did three-and-a-half-year-old Sally, who, when being put to bed by her grandmother, said in a serious tone, "When I grow into a big girl, I will miss myself."

CHAPTER EIGHT

The imaginary and the real

In the previous chapter, we saw how nursery age children are beginning to move from literal to more symbolic thinking and understanding. In this chapter, my focus is on the imagination, that is, the child's world of fantasy. Imagination, for the most part, is a valuable asset. Paradoxically, at the same time the world of fantasy develops, so does the child's capacity to test out and know the real world.

Developing imagination is vital for the growing child in that it shows a mind that is expanding and elaborating, making distinctions and is therefore becoming enriched. The capacity for imagination shows itself in the child's play, and in his creativity i.e. daydreams, the very things he makes, the stories he constructs. Some children possess fertile imaginations. Parents may need to act as mediators between fantasy and reality, helping to ensure that their children do not become overwhelmed by their excitement or anxieties. Other children may have poor imaginations; parents may then play a role in encouraging the development of ideas and in extending play, by initiating exploration and inviting the child to join in with the thinking. Imagination can provide avenues for self-expression and self-discovery; it can also be used as compensation for the harsh realities that some children find themselves in. Flights of fancy may have an unreal quality about them, but they may also contain an ingredient of hope.

The nursery age child frequently works on his predominant everyday conflicts by turning to the world of his imagination; for example, the four-year-old boy who insists on wearing his Superman outfit on his trip to the supermarket with his family, is finding a way of expressing his masculinity, his wish to be admired by mother and father, as well as showing his rivalrous feelings towards his stronger dad and his brothers.

Similarly, the little girl who chooses to wear wings and carry a wand, pretending to be a fairy, may be expressing her desire to be admired, to be looked at, and to captivate the attention of her Daddy and so become the favourite, most valued little girl, even a princess, in the family.

Children who live in difficult circumstances sometimes make use of their imagination to compensate for and to enrich their worlds, for example, by imagining a whole other universe where dreams come true; perhaps where Mummies and Daddies do not ever quarrel, or where there is a kind figure who comes to transform the family situation by offering just the right kind of help. Indeed, many fairy tales represent this theme, where children discover, through the facilitation of a helpful figure or messenger, their own skills and ways of changing or overcoming their dilemmas. Cinderella, or Jack in Jack and the Beanstalk are two such classic examples. A more contemporary figure is Willy Wonka in Roald Dahl's *Charlie and the Chocolate Factory*.

Parents may become concerned that a child is too caught up in the world of his imagination. For example:

Four-year-old Amy, who insisted she, too, was pregnant like her Mummy, and that the baby was due in the same week as her mother's. She spent a good deal of time talking to the baby she imagined was inside her tummy. The parents were worried by the forcefulness of her belief and indeed that the little girl would be very disappointed and upset when the mother's baby arrived. To their surprise, however, when the new real baby did arrive, the little girl seemed to have completely abandoned her fantasy state of "motherhood" and became absorbed in the reality of getting to know her new sibling. One might say that her imaginary pregnancy prepared Amy to welcome and accept the new addition to the family.

Winnicott writes in his book *The Child, the Family, and the Outside World* (1964) that the child of two, three, and four is in two worlds at once. We should not insist, when we are dealing with a child of that age, on an exact perception of the external world, as the boundaries between the two realms are not clear-cut for the child. The interplay between the two worlds can lead to much creativity. The adult's role in fostering the child's creative capacities is illustrated by Winnicott, when he writes,

> A child's feet need not be all the time firmly planted on the earth. If a little girl wants to fly we do not just say "Children don't fly". Instead of that we pick her up and carry her around over our heads and put her down on top of the cupboard, so she feels to have flown like a bird to her nest". [*ibid.*, p. 70]

Some nursery age children may turn to their own resources to deal with their anxieties about new situations. Imagination may provide the stimulus to discovering such resources.

> Four-year-old Jasmine was travelling on the ferry with her parents. This was her first time on a ferry; at first she was a little worried about the sensation of being on the ferry, especially when the boat seemed to move and judder. She asked her father what the rings hanging on the wall were for. He answered that they were there in case something happened to the ferry and people needed to get off it, explaining that the rings were there to help people stay afloat in the water. She listened. Later, she appeared in front of her older sister and her mother sporting a naval cap and assuming an air of authority. Jasmine was pretending to be the captain of the ferry. She walked around the ferry pretending to be the captain, in an imaginative attempt to actively master her fears during the channel crossing.

However, it is important for the child to gradually discover for himself how to separate the two worlds of imagination and reality: indeed, that they can be separated. Sometimes, children of this age become so carried away in the thrill of play that the monsters they are pretending to be suddenly take on a reality and the play breaks down, with the children becoming frightened and even crying. Play can be exciting and frightening and the boundary between the imaginary and the real is precarious when the imagination takes over and overwhelms the little child's mind. At such moments, the parents or the teacher may have to help to restore safety and calm the child. The adult may need to show the child the difference between the real and the imagined. The parent may need to draw the line between fantasy and action, as in the example below.

> Lucy, aged three years and eight months, was pretending to be a ghost. She had placed an old tablecloth over her, having made holes for her eyes, nose, and mouth. Lucy pranced around, making deep "whoo-ooing" sounds and surprising her brother and sister by jumping out at them from unexpected hiding places. She was becoming more and more excited and delighted by others' reactions to her "appearance". Then Lucy screamed and burst into tears. Her mother came to comfort her and asked what was the matter. It emerged that Lucy had caught sight of herself in the mirror, and, for a moment, given herself a tremendous fright.

The boundary between play and reality had temporarily broken down for Lucy. She had got so absorbed in her play that she lost herself, that is, her sense of identity, when she saw "the ghost" in the mirror. What she had been experiencing as fun very rapidly changed into something dangerously real. She needed her mother to help her find her real self again and to explain what had happened.

Children are often compared to sponges in that they soak up what they hear, mishear, and half understand. Sometimes, children of this age absorb the feelings that accompany messages or communication.

> For example, four-year-old Dave listened intently to his father's telling him about acid rain. The boy picked up on the sense of the world as a dangerous place and eventually, in this atmosphere of intellectually induced fear, he became burdened by such knowledge. And he became afraid of going out in the rain. His father thought he was educating his son; he did not realize that he was frightening Dave. He did not shield the boy enough, and the end result was that Dave became very frightened. The rain, which for so many children of this age is something they love to run out in and experience, instead became associated with danger, burning, and something to be avoided. Dave told me some of

THE IMAGINARY AND THE REAL

his fantasies about acid rain; acid rain can burn you, it smelt funny, and he did not want the rain on his skin.

It is likely that Dave's dad, similar to many parents, did not realize how much his son was taking his words literally. For Dave, all rain became acid, strange and dangerous. It might have been helpful for his father to spell out the specific situations where he might be affected and where he would not. With some nursery aged children, particularly those with vivid imaginations, the parent may need to be aware of changes in her child's behaviour in the direction of fearfulness or over-excitement. The parent may need to think back—was it something I said? The child in turn may benefit from help in unravelling "what did I think about it?" Sometimes, it may not be the very words themselves that trigger the child's reactions. The tone of the parent's voice, her mood and the general atmosphere of the conversation may be picked up by the young child and have an impact on his own feelings and behaviour.

Imaginary friends: a particular instance of the profound reality of the nursery age child's imagination

The world of imagination can also be turned to for social needs. Some children conjure up pretend friends who can be very important. What I mean by such a pretend or imaginary friend is a character who cannot be seen, but who has a definite vital existence in the child's mind. The imaginary friend is not a real living person with whom the child is pretending to be friends.

Parents sometimes get worried about children losing the distinction between fact and fantasy. Some parents describe feeling that things have gone too far, that some limit has been exceeded; for example, the child who demands that the imaginary friend come on holiday, too, as well as have a seat on the plane and a suitcase of his own. From the child's perspective, why shouldn't his friend come along for the holiday? After all, that's what friends are for.

The creative parent who senses the child's need for his pretend friend may find a creative solution, such as sharing space in the suitcase. However, some boundaries do need to be drawn—as with the plane seat—otherwise the parent runs the danger of being drawn too much into the world of make-believe. And it is this capacity to move between the worlds of the real and the unreal that is one of the central tasks that the preschool child is working towards.

It used to be thought that only lonely children created imaginary friends (Taylor, 1999). Now, we know that there are many reasons why children have such friends. Also, it is not only very intelligent children who create pretend friends (*ibid.*). Imaginary friends may appear at times of change and upheaval in a child's life, for example, moving home, parental separation, divorce or remarriage, and around times of the birth of siblings and the death of close relatives. Such imaginary friends stay for as long as they are needed emotionally. They then become incorporated into other aspects of the child's mind and are less overtly present. The friend becomes an inner character rather than an external presence whose existence is insisted on by the child.

Nursery age children may blame their imaginary friends for their own misdemeanours: "She ate the biscuit, not me!!" Imaginary friends may carry the more mischievous aspects of the child. Children who have a low opinion of their own attractiveness or intelligence may create very pretty or very clever imaginary friends as a way of boosting their self-esteem. Sometimes, as the child grows in his confidence in his attractiveness or intelligence, he leans less on his imaginary friends. They may be mentioned less, or just suddenly become something of the past.

These invisible friends are very real and special to the young child and need respectful handling by adults and, to some extent, siblings. There is a story from the Hampstead War Nurseries (Freud & Burlingham, 1944) in which a group of children who were living away from their parents, often with absent fathers fighting in the war, were on an outing and had just crossed the zebra crossing. One little girl stood still, refusing to move on. She insisted that everyone wait until her imaginary friend had also crossed the road. Everyone obliged!

CHAPTER NINE

The sense of "I" and self-esteem

T he building of a sense of "I", of identity, is a lifelong task. Some of the earliest foundations of this "I" have been laid down in the first two years of life in the interaction between parents and infant, and parents and toddler.

Self esteem is the value that the child has of himself, how well or badly he regards himself. Both the sense of identity and the sense of inner confidence which is part of self esteem are closely intertwined with relationships, with the attitudes of important others around, and with the child's sense of his growing body. The parent who encourages her child to try new experiences and who invites her child to express his feelings, helps her child to develop healthy self-esteem. Genuine words of praise from his parent can motivate a child and make him feel that his efforts are valued. The parent also helps her child by drawing the line, keeping firm limits and an eye on safety. By safety, I mean not only physical safety, but also the parent's providing an atmosphere in which her child can learn through making mistakes and in which her child can enjoy discovering what he can understand and do. Nursery school age children can draw enormous comfort and reassurance from knowing that a parent is present who is aware and engaged. Of course, parents cannot be available 100% of the time; but it is the child's sense of the parent's availability and his memories of experiences of his parent being tuned in to him that are key to the child's sense of his own value. Neither chaos (that is, anything goes) nor rigidity (that is, overly strict rules and lack of flexibility) contribute to an atmosphere of safety and self-confidence for the growing child.

A chaotic style of parenting can lead to a child feeling unprotected at a time when he is still learning to protect himself and cannot do it single-handed. A rigid style can lead to feelings of being over-controlled, and can make the child feel that his parents do not trust his abilities, which can then lead to doubts and lowering of his self-esteem. A lack of flexibility may curb spontaneity, and altogether the child may react to a rigid style by becoming fearful, even narrow-minded and unwilling to try out new situations and to venture beyond the familiar. Other children may rebel against the rigid style. They may sense the anxiety which underlies the rigidity. Such insecurity in the child may then lead to his testing out the parents' state of mind. This testing out can be taken by the parents to be a confirmation of the need for them to be rigid. Parents can help the situation by being aware of the resulting vicious circle they are both creating and being caught up in.

Children are finding a place in their family, comparing themselves with family members. Children of this age are becoming increasingly aware of their bodies and their gender identity. Preschool children are grappling with the ideas that we are not all the same, and discovering that mummies and daddies, and girls and boys have different shaped and made bodies.

> Three-and-a-half-year-old Margaret was puzzled when she saw her dad without his clothes. She asked her mother, "Mummy, why has daddy got a handle on his bottom?"

> Five-year-old Russell developed an interest in women's breasts. He sometimes imagined that he had breasts. He would stand in front of a mirror cupping his hands over his chest and sticking out his chest so that he looked as if he had breasts.

Nursery age children often become very curious and extremely aware, if not on the lookout for a sight, of their parents' and siblings' bodies. In many families, nudity is a casual matter; in others, the subject is surrounded by a strong sense of privacy. Some children become more than curious; they may be moving towards states of over-excitement. Such states can be unhelpful in that they may cause confusion and over-stimulate the imagination. The parent may need to intervene to calm down her child and perhaps find an opportune time when they can explore his questions and thoughts about being naked and seeing people in the nude.

There must be an enormous number of experiences of exploring him/herself and those who are part of his/her world before a child comes to realize that he/she is a boy or a girl. Anatomical parts play a large role in this process, but it is likely that the child perceives the body parts in conjunction with his feelings about the person concerned. The presence or absence of a penis is likely to be linked to the position taken for urinating by each parent, much as the size of the breasts may be linked to observations of a new sibling. The child has to struggle to learn that, besides anatomical features, there is a multitude of functions and roles that characterize each specific gender.

Discovering these elements of himself and those in his world leads the child, for example, to question "How was I made?" and to absorb the complex relationship between his parents and how they relate to him. Closeness to each parent, feelings of rivalry or competition with them, learning to accept his position in the family, are all enormously important steps in constructing the child's sense of self as "boy" or "girl" with which he will move into the wider world.

The desire to be a girl or boy, that is, the opposite gender, may appear in drawings and in fantasy play, and is quite common at this age. Little boys sometimes express their wish to be girls by waddling about, having "grown" fat with cushions in pretence of being pregnant. They can alternate between rough play, literally throwing the cushion baby to one another, and more tender play, where they show a nurturing and/or protective attitude towards the imagined baby.

Little girls may show their desire to be boys by playing witches flying on broomsticks, expressing, *inter alia*, their wish for what boys have. Some girls at playtime in the nursery insert long objects into their knickers and then strut around, pretending to be boys, sometimes announcing "Look what I've got".

Young children need help in developing confidence in their being a little boy or little girl; parents can play a crucial role by providing genuine praise and admiration.

Children are thinking about the differences between the genders, as revealed below in Jake's joke and the reactions of his nursery school mates.

> The children are putting on their aprons, which they wear while eating lunch. There are two varieties of patterned apron; striped ones and flowered ones. Jake (four years and three months old) points at Jimmy's apron, then Carlo's, then his own, remarking that they have all got stripes. Susie says, "I haven't." Jake says, "You've got flowers; flowers are stripes for girls." Susie laughs, followed by the three boys (Davids, 1987, p. 315).

I was struck by Jake's diplomacy and awareness of sex differences as well as his sure and surprising use of the condensed symbol that seemed to elicit the laughter.

The young child's wish to take the place of one parent is urgent and passionate. When such wishes are thwarted, rage and frustration may manifest themselves.

> Five-year-old Mike was very keen on his older sister's female friend. They sometimes played kings and queens together. One day the little boy held out a Plasticine ring which he had made, and earnestly asked her, "Will you marry me?" When she said she could not really marry him, he asked her why. She explained that when he was bigger he would find someone else. He retorted indignantly, " I no wait. I want now."

Sometimes the child can place his passionate wish to displace the rival in the future, as did three-and-a-half-year-old Holly, who said, "When I grow up, I can sit in the front seat; and when Mummy gets smaller she will have to sit in the car-seat."

The child may hold a strong conviction that the same sex parent will no longer be there, as illustrated by four-year-old Amy, who announced to her dad that she intended marrying him one day. When he asked "But what about mummy?", she answered that she would no longer be there. She simply removed the competition.

The earnest, heartfelt tone of the children in the above examples was met by amusement from their parents. Holly's mother laughed in response to her remark, and Amy's dad joked with her about mummy's "disappearance". Such fantasies are virtually universal, and are not early warning signals of future hostile or cruel impulses. Parents should not regard them with alarm. Joking about such wishes with the child may be helpful to the child, while being careful not to laugh at the child or joke at his expense.

One senses the power of the young child's personality and her mother's forbearance in the following example.

> A four-and-a-half-year-old, curly-haired girl was walking behind her mother and older brother in my street. She was clutching the long ears of her toy rabbit while she screamed at the top of her lungs, "I don't like walking." As she walked she kept up her verbal protest. Her mother and brother kept walking. Her mother looked over her shoulder, saying, "You're going to see Daddy." This made no difference to the girl's loud protest. Her mother said, "Oh well, we'll get a taxi." There was a brief pause. Her mother held her hand. Her brother then tried to get close to mother. His younger sister pushed him out with determined force. She then started her rageful cry again, "I don't like walking." At times he looked back at her as she clung on to her rabbit's ears and protested at the top of her lungs while she walked. The threesome kept on walking; they did not hail a taxi.

> I was struck by her energy. I was amused by the inherent paradox—I don't like walking but I am walking. The little girl was grappling with the compromise, with the painful relinquishment of having her way, with the realization that I do not like doing what I have to. I sensed her wish to be carried rather than making the effort of walking. The rivalry with her older brother seemed to add to her fury, yet she held her own ground. I could not help admiring her strength of character and how she was expressing herself with her whole being in this situation.

This happened in a public place. Mother kept in contact with her, looking over her shoulder and withstanding her daughter's stormy protest. Mother held her hand. Mother did not stop her daughter's protest, but neither did she allow her protest to derail them in the achievement of their task. Mother's quiet forbearance was as impressive as her daughter's passionate protest. The attitude and presence of this mother, as well as that of the father in the following example, are illustrative of the sense of attunement which is key to the child's self-esteem described at the beginning of this chapter.

The little boy in the next example was patiently handled by his dad.

> I noticed a family on the busy morning tube who appeared to be en route for their vacation. Mother was standing behind the pram with a younger child. Father was standing next to his son of about four and a half years old. The boy was clearly very excited, and communicated his state of mind to his dad. The little boy clambered up on the ventilated slot and squatted there, looking rather like a monkey. His dad stood nearby, minding that his son did not lose his balance. His son announced loudly," I don't like this seat; I'd like a proper one like those people." His dad laughed and stroked his arm. Then someone vacated one of the fold-down seats and the boy quickly sat on it. He looked pleased with himself. His dad pointed to the tube map and explained that there were three more stations before they needed to change trains. When the train reached the next stop, the boy said, "Is it three or two?"; his dad counted with him on his hands and at the next stop the boy tried to use his hands to work it out.

What is striking about this situation is the father's receiving the boy's mood and his calm watchfulness of the boy's perch. The father was helping to build the boy's confidence and expand his sense of discovery and understanding of the world around him. He handled a potentially uncomfortable situation by saving face for the boy, protecting him, but not overly so. The father's amusement at his son's remark was appropriate. Indeed, the young boy said what many people, and perhaps his father as well, were thinking. One senses how much this boy was taking in of this new experience. Here, father was very much facilitating this child's understanding and management of a potentially frustrating and tiring situation.

Sometimes, the important people in the child's world are there to quietly witness the child's awareness of their own attractiveness.

> After watching the princess in *Star Wars*, three-year-old Lara told her grandmother, "There is the princess. She is beautiful, just like me."

The grandmother sensitively allowed her granddaughter to compliment herself with aplomb, which at this age can be so necessary for building a strong sense of identity and self-worth.

CHAPTER TEN

The world of relationships

The quality of nursery age children's relationships is changing, both within the family and beyond the family, as they get to know other children and adults in the community. Going to nursery school introduces the child to a wider world, to children of different cultures and children who come from families that have different ways and mores. The nursery school may be the child's first experience of a group of children of similar age. He is faced with the challenge of finding a place in a group of similarly aged children. The experience of having to share nursery school staff with many others may also raise anxieties. This is especially so in children who come from small families and who are used to more exclusive attention. Children in single parent families, or in families where another language is spoken, may also face anxieties about being in a group that they may experience as too large or as strange.

However, there are also many wonderful opportunities that come with broadening one's social circle. Children can be stimulated and enriched by other children's ideas and different perspectives. Gradually, play with other children facilitates the development of empathy, an ability to appreciate situations and experiences from others' points of view. Dramatic play and swapping of roles can encourage empathy. The child can experience what it feels like to be, for example, the leader and the follower. He begins to view the world and interpersonal situations in a less egocentric manner, that is, according to his needs and desires. He begins to be more of a companion to other children, a partner in making up games and roles. Nursery age children sometimes choose playmates on the basis of a shared common interest, that is, enjoying washing and dressing dolls, or becoming Power Rangers or mighty knights to the rescue, or playing dressing up in a more secluded place, such as under the stairs or in a corner.

It is very important for parents to take time to investigate the schools that their child might attend. Apart from feeling that the school has the right atmosphere for their particular child, parents need to make sure that there is good communication and a sense of trust between the school staff and themselves. Such a sense of trust is essential in facilitating the confident development of the child at home and at school.

The feeling of belonging to a nursery school may form an important part of a child's identity. Sitting in a circle listening to a story read by the teacher, and participating in giving one's reaction, can be a fun, new experience. Alongside the possibilities of creative co-operation, there are, of course, the thornier issues of competition. Some children struggle to take turns, to bear the frustration of waiting, and struggle to bear not being the one and only star. Others may prefer to be quiet and be in the background, finding the situation of being encouraged to participate new and scary. Some children prefer to bide their time. There are many different ways of joining a group that are neither signs of severe difficulty nor permanent ways of behaving.

Playtime at nursery school may change from excited co-operation among two or three children to sudden scenes of explosions of emotions where the help of an adult is needed. Suddenly, what is fun has collapsed, with a child weeping about being hurt or about an injustice that has occurred. These situations offer the opportunity for children to be helped to look at their contribution to the breakdown of the game. Their understanding of one another may gradually grow. And they also learn not only how to cope with their own sense of being bruised emotionally, but sometimes learn ways of mending relationships when they go wrong.

At nursery school, children learn to play the roles required by games, from the simplest games of catch to playing families. They learn versatility and widen their perspectives; they may need to be encouraged by the school staff, as some children are less adventurous and tend to choose the same role repeatedly: for example, always the baby, or the ghost. It is valuable for parents to show interest in their child's attitude in school, since it is helpful if such observations are shared by teachers and parents. Parents may have some ideas as to the reasons why the child tends to pick a certain part or character; they might wonder aloud about the child's preference and wait to hear what he says.

Young children need predictability. They often love the schedule of the nursery school day or half-day. The outer structure of the pattern of their day can help them house their wilder natures and impulses so that they can exercise self-control and thereby build a sense of self-esteem. Withdrawn children may need encouragement to come out of their shells. Although the parent cannot protect the child from uncertainty, she can prepare the child for new experiences. She can talk about nursery school, describe it, show the child where it is, and go with him to visit. Similarly, experiences such as going to the dentist or doctor, moving house, or going on holiday can be talked about in advance. Such discussions can help the child imagine what he is about to encounter. He may have questions about the doctor or the new house. Knowing that his questions are welcomed, that he can ask his parent, helps to diminish his confusion and anxieties. Through such preparations, the child can feel more in control and is more equipped to master new experiences. The parent can play a crucial role in being there to share in her child's feelings and thoughts. The parent's willingness to understand and listen contributes to making what may feel unpredictable less overwhelming.

Nursery age children experience time in a subjective, emotional manner. Adults can help children with their sense of time. By making markers showing measures of time or distance, as with the boy and his dad on the tube (Chapter Nine), time becomes both meaningful and manageable. Otherwise, a wait can feel interminable and arbitrary. Gradually, the child can learn a sense of time, space, and distance. The father who is more attuned to his son shows the boy the map. It is interesting that on long-haul flights these days, a map is projected showing the passengers where their plane is in relation to the point of departure and the ultimate destination.

Children of three to five are really coming to terms with living with and in a family. The realization that the parents have their own separate special relationship which one cannot be part of, or, indeed, destroy, is a momentous set of realizations that the child comes to terms with over time. I would say that one of the primary achievements is the realization of, and making an adaptation to, finding oneself in a triadic relationship. Mummy is daddy's love. There may be strong rivalry between mother and daughter over prettiness, and the little girl may feel bitter jealousy of her father's special gifts and attention to mother.

Older siblings may be viewed with admiration and envy; older siblings can be very protective and stimulating to their younger sisters and brothers. They can act as spurs to the younger siblings' development.

Grandparents often enjoy a special relationship with their nursery age grandchildren. They are a step away from the child, as they do not carry the responsibility of the parent, and this perhaps frees them to resemble older playmates. Grandparents sometimes joke that they can go home when things get difficult and leave the grandchildren to their parents. This fits in with the child's casting the grandparents in a benign light; they may be seen by the children as allies who can empathize with the wish to carry on playing despite the rules set by their parents.

Grandparents may recognize much of themselves in their grandchildren: "I was just like that when I was his age." This may lead to amusement and to a tendency to empathize when the grandchild meets similar experiences that the grandparent encountered as a young child. Buried memories may come to light again for the grandparents.

Grandchildren can be a source of much pride and pleasure to their grandparents. To the preschool child, the grandparent may be a figure of curiosity. Often, children inquire what the grandparents did at their age. Were their parents strict, too? Did they play the same games? Children are often fascinated by stories told by their grandparents of their childhood. Children sometimes relish stories of their parents' childhood as remembered and told by their grandparents. Grandparents may, therefore, provide a sense of continuity between the generations in that they are carriers of the family history. Children may draw a sense of being valued and cherished by their grandparents; this can form a key ingredient of their self-esteem. For grandparents, grandchildren may be seen as a legacy and as representing the future.

Nursery age children are developing the capacity to relate to peers and older children in the nuclear family, the wider family, and at school. They are deepening their understanding of their siblings so that they can live and grow alongside them. They are learning the crucial value of both intimacy and solitude.

The next observation illustrates the play of two siblings.

It is a summer afternoon. Julie and her brother Tommy are playing; there is about one year difference between them. She, about five, is holding her rag-doll while they have drinks with the family. The two children are engaged with one another. Four-year-old Tommy is the more agile of the two. Julie is putting her doll into her little stroller; I notice in the background that her mother is holding a small baby. The little girl talks to her doll, tucks her into the stroller with much care, and then, it seems, out of the corner of her eye, watches her brother jumping and climbing near a tree. Julie turns the stroller around and then abandons it temporarily. She follows her brother's jumping from one stump to another; every now and again she looks at the stroller, as if she is checking its whereabouts and reassuring herself that her doll is still there. Julie then follows her brother, who appears excited and wants to show her something behind the bushes. Then she comes back and picks up her doll, gently straightens out the doll's clothes and goes to sit down, holding the doll in the crook of her arm, looking rather dreamy. Julie looks rather maternal and she comes across as protective and proud of her little one. Julie's dreaminess is not disturbed by Tommy's rather boisterous banging of a long stick he has discovered. He walks up and down, displaying his new find. Tommy seems to want his sister's attention and shows his annoyance by calling out to her every now and again. Julie seems rather oblivious and caught up in the contentment of her own world.

The children are aware of one another and move between their own preoccupations and shared play. The boy shows little interest in mother's baby. Tommy derives pleasure from moving his body and through physical exploration of his environment. He seems to be venturing out and returning with his finds, which he wants to display and have admired. Julie has some interest in Tommy's explorations, but her fundamental interest seems to lie in her playing mother to her doll baby. Julie keeps her "baby" in mind while she joins her brother in physical activity; she is perhaps identified with her mother's capacity to keep at least two children in mind.

Through relationships, the child augments his sense of his identity and his sense of the other. He no longer solely relates to other children on the basis of what needs they can fulfil; he is becoming more aware of individual children's unique qualities and talents. He begins to recognize what he shares with others and how he differs. As illustrated by Julie and Tommy in the example above, play moves from play alongside to play together to moments of solitary play.

CHAPTER ELEVEN

Big school

The prospect of entering primary school is an important moment in the development of the child and his parents. Anxiety, excitement, pride, and doubt may all accompany this next step for parent and child.

Not only is the child broadening his experiences of the world by entering a new educational and social system, but the parents are also expanding their social circle by getting to know other parents. Parents may find themselves feeling a new competitiveness with others, drawing comparisons with how other children are developing. Some parents may feel judged by others in unhelpful ways: for example, being considered lax or too strict in discipline. Other parents may seek and find solace in hearing other parents' experiences and dilemmas, and come to see the new circle as supportive. It can be most reassuring to know you are not the only mum who has lain awake feeling both excited and worried about how you and your daughter will deal with the first few weeks of "big school".

Expectations and anxieties from their own early school experiences may come alive again for parents. The parent may confuse her own experiences with those of her child. She may assume that her child will follow the same course as she herself did. She may need to become aware of such blurring in order to hear and see her child's own reactions. Similarly, distinctions and differences between siblings' reactions need to be allowed for: for example, that older brother Jack may have been cautious and shy in the first few weeks of big school, whereas Danny seems enthusiastic and to be enjoying the new setting.

Parents may find themselves responding in different ways to the new challenge. Some may want to rush their child and adopt a pushing approach. Others may withdraw from their child, not wanting to interfere or get in the way of the child's more independent strides. Some parents may feel such a degree of sympathy with their child's experience, feel so in it together, that they struggle to step back and gradually let go of their child.

This is where teachers can be very helpful in identifying the specific child's needs and thinking about approaches that would facilitate his entry into school. Teachers are aware that parents themselves are going through another transition in a further letting go of their maturing child. Some parents are taken aback by the strength of their own feelings of loss. Mothers talk about feeling that it is the end of an era, that they feel they have lost their nursery aged little child, who is now disappearing into the "big school" crowd. The entry into primary school may also be welcomed, as it provides a longed-for breathing space for the parents.

Choosing a primary school bears many similarities to the selection of an appropriate nursery school. Parents need to feel that they can communicate with the staff, and that they can safely entrust their child to the school team. Other factors influencing choice of school may depend on the parents' knowledge of their particular child with his individual character and needs: for example, a child who loves physical activity, would blossom in a school where sports and/or dance is clearly valued and encouraged. The choice of a big school is a significant step; the nursery school is usually smaller and has a cosier, more familiar atmosphere. Big school has a hierarchy, many layers of older children, and physically the place is usually larger. The young child, especially if he does not have an older brother or sister, may find the presence of older children foreign.

He may meet children who speak a range of different languages, who come from unfamiliar cultures and practise hitherto unknown religions. One of the most obvious differences between nursery school and "big" school is the size of the actual place, the numbers of children, and the staff–pupil ratio. The child may feel overwhelmed by the idea of being one among so many others. Teachers are usually well aware of such fears. Parents can help to ease their children's transition and adjusting by naming the worries and the excitement, answering questions as the child asks them, and generally helping the child through the changes during the first weeks and months.

Sometimes, anxieties about separation can recur for the child. The parent needs to work with the teacher on how best to manage such experiences for the particular child. It helps if there is a co-ordinated approach; clear messages can help the child know what is expected of him both at home and school, and by teacher and parent. Settling in may take time and be characterized by ups and downs. The parent may have to work on herself not to become too alarmed by what she may see as backward steps, such as clingy behaviour or bossiness. Such backward moves may all be part of the process of the child's adapting to his new place.

The child faces different expectations in his new school. In nursery school, the boundaries between work and play are usually more fluid. Now the work starts to become more task-orientated. The teacher may be perceived as stricter and more demanding. The child may miss his nursery schoolteacher who felt more intimate and familiar, as did Alice (see p. 16). Some children struggle to find satisfaction in more formal learning, rather than play for play's sake. For example, learning to read requires much attention and repetition. The child is faced with the struggle, the effort, and the grind. Formal learning can be exciting and fill the young child with experiences of achievement. But it can also confront the child, yet again, with the realization that things do not come immediately and that he does not know everything. The child once again faces frustrations and failures, and may need encouragement from his parent to continue in the face of setbacks. With these realizations comes the deepening of patience and the lengthening of persistence.

Continued opportunities for play are essential to balance the pressures of the new, more formal learning. Indeed, there is much current debate about how young children learn best. A submission to a recent review of primary education by the National Primary

Headteachers' Association (reported in the *Observer*, 7 October 2007) said that a playful approach to teaching seemed "to disappear entirely in the majority of schools as soon as children entered year one", regardless of the fact that those born in the summer months had just turned five. The chair of the association advocates that children learn better when they enjoy. He believes that guided play is the best way for younger children to be taught, and recommends that it be maintained in the classroom until children are at least six.

Parents may need to provide opportunities outside school, such as dance, music, art, or drama, to balance the input and ethos of the school, particularly in this time when schools have become more target-orientated and seem to have lost some of the opportunities for the facilitation of the young child's imagination.

REFERENCES

Bowlby, J. (1988). *A Secure Base: Clinical Applications of Attachment Theory*. London: Routledge.

Cole, B. (1993). *Mummy Laid an Egg*. London: Random House Children's Books.

Coles, P. (2006). *Sibling Relationships*. London: Karnac.

Davids, J. (1987). Laughter in the nursery. *Bulletin of the Anna Freud Centre, 10*: 307–318.

Finding Nemo (2003). Film. Burbank: Walt Disney Pictures.

Freud, A. (1967). About losing and being lost. In: *The Writings of Anna Freud*, Volume IV (pp. 302–316). New York: International Universities Press.

Freud, A., & Burlingham, D. (1944). *Infants Without Families*. New York: International Universities Press.

Freud, S. (1905d). *Three Essays on the Theory of Sexuality. S.E., 7*: 125–243. London: Hogarth.

McBratney, S., & Jeram, A. (1994). *Guess How Much I Love You*. London: Walker, 2001.

Mitchell, J. (2003). *Siblings*. Cambridge: Polity Press.

Paley, V. G. (2004). *A Child's Work*. Chicago, IL: University of Chicago Press.

Provence, S., & Solnit, A. J. (1983). Development-promoting aspects of the sibling experience. *Psychoanalytic Study of the Child, 38*: 337–351.

Ross, T. (2001). *I Want A Sister*. Hammersmith: Collins.

Taylor, M. (1999). *Imaginary Companions and the Children Who Create Them*. New York: Oxford University Press.

Waddell, M., & Firth, B. (1988). *Can't You Sleep, Little Bear?* London: Walker.

Waddell, M., & Benson, P. (1992). *Owl Babies*. London: Walker.

Winnicott, D. W. (1936). Mental hygiene of the pre-school child. In: R. Shepherd, J. Johns, & H. Taylor Robinson (Eds.), *D. W. Winnicott Thinking About Children* (pp. 59–76). London: Karnac, 1996.

Winnicott, D. W. (1964). *The Child, The Family, and the Outside World*. Harmondsworth: Penguin.